OFFICIAL REPORT

OF THE

THIRTY - SIXTH INTERNATIONAL

CONVENTION OF CHRISTIAN

ENDEAVOR

Held at Grand

Rapids, Michigan

July 8 - 13, 1937

First Fruits Press
Wilmore, Kentucky
c2015

First Fruits Press
The Academic Open Press of Asbury Theological Seminary
204 N. Lexington Ave., Wilmore, KY 40390
859-858-2236
first.fruits@asburyseminary.edu
asbury.to/firstfruits

The Official Report

OF THE

Thirty-Sixth

INTERNATIONAL CONVENTION

OF

CHRISTIAN ENDEAVOR

PROGRAM GUIDE
FOR SOCIETIES AND UNIONS

GRAND RAPIDS, MICHIGAN
July 8-13, 1937

Convention Recorder
CATHERINE MILLER BALM

Editors of the Official Report
BERT H. DAVIS
STANLEY B. VANDERSALL

Man's courage fails
dark fears appall,
The whole world rocks
while Kingdom's fall:
"Christ for the Crisis!"
now hear the call;
"Christ for the Crisis!"
The All in All!

The Message of President Roosevelt
THE WHITE HOUSE
WASHINGTON

July 1, 1937

DEAR DR. POLING:

When you gather with the International Society of Christian Endeavor and the World's Christian Endeavor Union in biennial convention in Grand Rapids please give all present an assurance of my sincere interest.

I note with satisfaction that in connection with this joint meeting the International Youth's Distinguished Service Award is to be conferred upon Rear Admiral Richard Evelyn Byrd in recognition of his achievements as an explorer at the world's Southernmost outpost. His is a career which should be an inspiration to youth everywhere and it is particularly fitting that he should receive the accolade of the International Society of Christian Endeavor and the World's Christian Endeavor Union.

I trust that the sessions in Grand Rapids will be fruitful of wise counsels in the interest of our young people. Sooner than many of us realize theirs will be the responsibility for the direction of affairs, and in the discharge of the tasks which will fall to them they will need, as the world has always needed, the spiritual strength and courage which come from reliance upon the everlasting reality of religion. In that spirit I wish for your gathering the fullest measure of success, and send to all who participate my hearty felicitations and warmest personal greetings.

Very sincerely yours

(*Signed*) FRANKLIN D. ROOSEVELT.

REVEREND DANIEL A. POLING, D D., LL.D.
President, International Society of Christian Endeavor,
Mount Vernon and Joy Streets,
Boston, Massachusetts

The Reply of Dr. Poling

His Excellency Franklin D. Roosevelt
The President of the United States
Washington, D. C.

The Thirty-sixth International Convention of the International
Society of Christian Endeavor is honored to receive your thoughtful
and generous message.

A vast throng of Christian young people, overflowing the great
auditorium, gathered from all over America, reciprocates your kind
wishes and pledges itself afresh to the ideals and principles of
Christian citizenship and world peace. It gives you the assurance
of its prayerful desire for your guidance and strength.

It is especially grateful for your tribute to Rear Admiral Byrd,
whom the Endeavor movement has been delighted to honor tonight.

(Signed) DANIEL A. POLING.

We Shall Always Honor
THE FOUNDERS

Doctor and Mrs. Francis E. Clark

On February 2, 1881, the first Christian Endeavor society was organized in the Williston Congregational Church, Portland, Maine.

Doctor Clark ceased his labors on May 26, 1927.

Mother Clark still lives usefully and influentially for all of Christian Endeavor.

Report of the Thirty-sixth International Convention of Christian Endeavor

Contents

Book 1

Chapter	Page
I. What Makes a Convention Great?	11
II. The Convention Begins	15
The Delegates Arrive—The Exhibition Hall—The Challenging Open Session—Admiral Byrd's Address on Peace	
III. Each Day Brings Its Gifts	31
Friday, Saturday, Sunday, and the State Conventions of Michigan, Indiana, and Wisconsin on Monday	
IV. Pages from a Delegate's Diary	39
Monday	
V. We Face the Future	47
Tuesday	
VI. We Hear Inspiring Addresses	55
Including the Addresses of Dr. Poling, Dr. Evans, Dr. Peale. Extracts from the Addresses of Dr. Norwood and Bishop Kyles. Brief Statements Worth Pondering, by Several Speakers	
VII. Questions Asked and Answered in the Radio Conference	75
The Holy Communion Service	78
VIII. We Worship	81
IX. Forward Steps in Organization	83
X. We Enjoy Good Fellowship	85
XI. What Happened in the Educational Conferences	93

XII. JUNIOR FEATURES IN THE CONVENTION . . 103

XIII. OUR RESOLUTIONS 117

XIV. WHO'S WHO IN THE GRAND RAPIDS COMMITTEE 125

Book 2

A PROGRAM GUIDE FOR CHRISTIAN ENDEAVOR SOCIETIES AND INTERDENOMINATIONAL UNIONS

I. CHRIST FOR EVERY CRISIS IN PERSONAL LIVING . 129

II. CHRIST FOR EVERY CRISIS IN COMMUNITY LIFE . 135

III. CHRIST FOR EVERY CRISIS IN NATIONAL LIFE . 142

IV. CHRIST FOR EVERY INTERNATIONAL CRISIS . 146

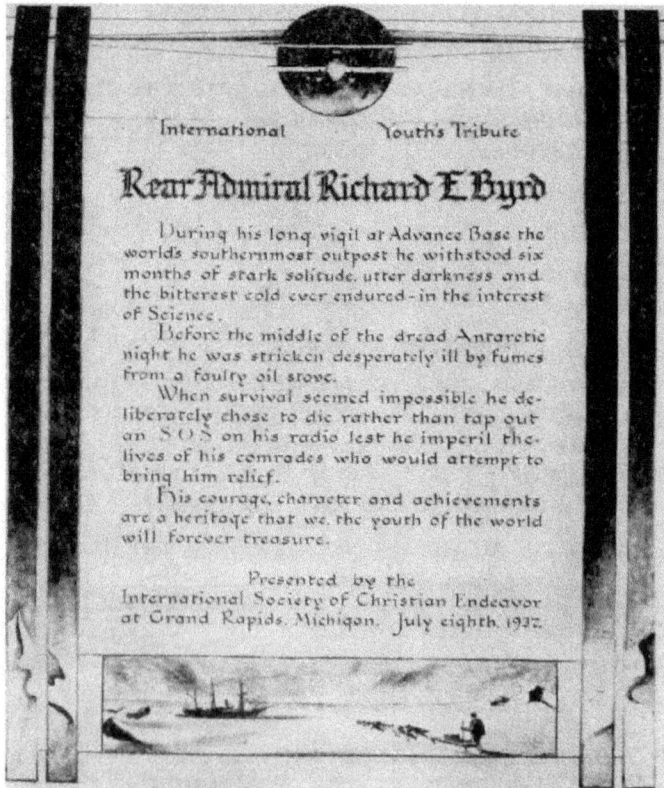

International Youth's Tribute

Rear Admiral Richard E Byrd

During his long vigil at Advance Base the world's southernmost outpost he withstood six months of stark solitude, utter darkness and the bitterest cold ever endured—in the interest of Science.

Before the middle of the dread Antarctic night he was stricken desperately ill by fumes from a faulty oil stove.

When survival seemed impossible he deliberately chose to die rather than tap out an SOS on his radio lest he imperil the lives of his comrades who would attempt to bring him relief.

His courage, character and achievements are a heritage that we, the youth of the world will forever treasure.

Presented by the
International Society of Christian Endeavor
at Grand Rapids, Michigan, July eighth, 1937.

THE BEAUTIFUL PARCHMENT SCROLL GIVEN TO ADMIRAL BYRD AS A CITATION BY PRESIDENT POLING

BOOK 1
The Official Report

OUR PRESENT LEADERS

in the Wide World of Christian Endeavor

Doctor and Mrs. Daniel A. Poling

Doctor Poling is President of the World's Christian Endeavor Union and of the International Society of Christian Endeavor.

I

What Makes a Convention Great?

Now that our hopes of "Grand Rapids, 1937" have become history and we *know* that the Thirty-Sixth International Convention of Christian Endeavor was indeed "a great convention," it is interesting for us to consider just what made this priceless experience possible for us.

A great convention never "just happens." What makes a great convention possible?

A great convention grows out of a great *purpose.* It begins growing long before the delegates come thronging into the convention city. The Grand Rapids Convention began to grow at the end of the Philadelphia Convention in 1935. "We Choose Christ!" decided the Endeavorers in Philadelphia. Dr. Poling and other leaders started at once to think of how the next convention could make that decision more meaningful in the lives of the youth of North America.

It was inevitable, in the face of national and world conditions, that for the Grand Rapids Convention the tremendous purpose should be—

"Christ for the Crisis!"

The realization of the purpose of a convention depends upon careful *planning* of every part of the convention program. How much time shall be spent listening to speeches? Who shall the speakers be and on what subjects shall they talk? What problems shall be discussed in the educational conferences? What organization methods recommended? Who shall lead the conferences? What special features shall be included in the program?

Careful planning by a committee under the direction of Dr. Harry Thomas Stock, made possible for the Grand Rapids Convention the most inspiring and stimulating program a Christian Endeavor convention has ever had.

But a program is valueless without people to participate in it, so enthusiastic *promotion* is necessary to make a convention great in numbers. Promotion of "Grand Rapids, 1937" was begun by those tireless secretaries of the International Society of Christian Endeavor, Dr. Stanley B. Vandersall and Mr. Carroll M. Wright. It was carried on energetically by the State field secretaries and by the volunteer officers of every State and county union. It was the earnest avocation of scores of individual Endeavorers. Numbers alone do not make a convention worth-while, but .t is cause for rejoicing that 8,000 registered delegates attended the Grand Rapids Convention.

No factor counts more in assuring the success of a convention than adequate local *preparation*. Seldom, if ever, in convention history has a local committee worked harder or more effectively to achieve perfection in the myriad details of a convention than did Mr. George Veldman's committee in Grand Rapids. In the provision of a cool and beautiful auditorium and classrooms, in hospitable entertainment with all sorts of delightful extra surprises, in the training of a notably fine choir, in the efficient organization of a corps of attractive and helpful ushers and pages, in the printing of an artistic and well-arranged program, in the enlisting of religious and civic groups to welcome and aid the delegates—in these and many other services our great-hearted hosts in Grand Rapids made the Convention memorable.

Hundreds of people worked for long months to make the 1937 Convention possible; thousands more who could have no share in the planning and preparation *prayed* with them that it would be blessed. On the afternoon before the Convention opened, early arrivals met to pray together. The attitude of those who prayed was expressed in this brief prayer of an Intermediate girl:

"Dear Father, as we come for the first time to a convention, help us to put much into it. Let us have a part in making it worth while so that there will be something for everyone to take back to his home and church. Amen."

It *was* a great convention, the Thirty-sixth International Convention of Christian Endeavor! A great purpose, careful planning, enthusiastic promotion, adequate local preparation and earnest prayer made its greatness possible. But those to whom it seemed most wonderful were those who came to it most humbly and unselfishly, seeking "to put much into it," "to have a part in making it worth-while."

THE GRAND RAPIDS CONVENTION IN SESSION

DR. HOWARD B. GROSE
Vice President, Emeritus

DR. WILLIAM HIRAM FOULKES
Vice President

DR. DANIEL A. POLING
President

HARRY N. HOLMES
Vice President

DR. A. E. CORY
Vice President

Officers of the International Society

II

The Convention Begins!

The Delegates Arrive

THE friendly invasion of Grand Rapids started several days before the Thirty-sixth International Convention of Christian Endeavor was officially declared "in session." Trustees of the International Society of Christian Endeavor, State Presidents and Denominational Directors of Young People's Work came early for long meetings devoted to the official business of Christian Endeavor. Delegates came early because they just simply couldn't wait for their Convention experiences to begin!

They came from homes thousands of miles apart. From Florida and Maine, from Mexico and Canada, from Hawaii and New Jersey and from all points between, came the eager hosts of young people. They came by many varied methods of transportation, in special trains, in chartered motor busses, in privately owned and generously crowded automobiles of every make and condition, by a combination of land and water travel, even on foot.

Jack Grosvenor of Iowa hitch-hiked from Council Bluffs. Albert Windle, blind from birth, hitch-hiked from Coatesville, Pennsylvania. He came to Grand Rapids early so that he could get acquainted with the city and help other delegates to find their way around it. And Ted Miller pedaled his bicycle four hundred miles from Toronto, Canada.

Some of the delegates wanted so much to come that no deficiency of funds could deter them. Boys from Washington, D. C., slept in their automobile until gracious people of Grand Rapids hospitably invited them into their home. The homes of Grand Rapids indeed were opened to hundreds of delegates, while others enjoyed the courtesy of Grand Rapids hotels. If three or four or even six shared a hotel room to cut down expenses that was not a resented economy. That was so much more fun!

The large State delegations arrived on July 8. So did a sizzling heat-wave! It was hot enough to wilt a salamander, but the spirits of the Endeavorers rose with the thermometer. Who could help being enthusiastic over a city which sent its best bands of music to meet the train-loads of visitors and escorted those visitors to their temporary homes as if they were visiting royalty or heroes of high adventure? The fact that a real hero *had* arrived, that all of us would see him and hear him speak that very night, increased the excitement.

Downtown Grand Rapids took on new color and brightness as the merchants hung out their welcoming red and white banners and the delegates appeared in their colorful costumes. Michigan Endeavorers wore shoulder capes over white dresses or suits and flat, coolie-type hats—red for Grand Rapids and blue and yellow for all outside of Grand Rapids. Delegates from Kansas were topped with mammoth sunflower hats, delegates from Iowa were gorgeous in crimson blouses, New Jersey youths were recognized by their orange and black regalia, Wisconsin Endeavorers identified by huge crimson chrysanthemums which fluttered on their white blouses. Color everywhere!

Laughter, too, and excited greetings. In the hotel lobbies, in the great area of Convention Hall devoted to "Registration" and "Information" and to the sale of books (we must come back to the book counters, their contents look particularly interesting!).

"Did you know that Illinois has the largest delegation that State ever sent to any International Convention?"

"Have you seen the bride and groom from Kansas?"

"Mother Clark is here! Really!"

"There will be fifty-three educational conferences, not counting those for Intermediates. I want to attend the one on 'Working for Peace.' "

"Jim! I haven't seen you since—was it the Milwaukee Convention?"

"I saw Admiral Byrd! I was as near—"

Exhibition Hall

It was quieter on the lower floor of Convention Hall. Here was the Exhibition Hall, not yet discovered by many delegates but later to be crowded with eager seekers after new ideas. Here with posters and pictures the State unions showed something of their many activities. Here the denominations offered helpful leaflets and pamphlets on young people's work and suggested practical ways in which Christian Endeavor work could be carried on in each denomination. Here the Canadian Christian Endeavor Union demonstrated the vast extent of its geographical boundaries and the goals it has set for its work. Here the Golden Rule Union (Negro) of Washington, D. C., displayed artistic proof of its continuing progress. Here mission boards showed pictures of fields ripe for harvest. Gigantic billboard posters, newspapers, and mimeographed materials illustrated the possibilities of giving publicity to Christian Endeavor.

The exhibition of the World's Christian Endeavor Union was especially significant. Societies and unions from far-off places had sent exhibits. There were silken banners from Korea and China. Australia and New Zealand had sent samples of their Christian Endeavor literature. Germany had sent posters showing the pledge in German and the badges and arm-bands used by German societies. These were collected by the missionary department of the Michigan Christian Endeavor Union.

We lingered a long while before the beautifully painted posters from India. Here was an exquisite piece of handwork, a pledge in the Telegu language, bordered with a lotus design copied from the stained-glass windows of the Jacob Chamberlain Memorial Church in Madanapalle, South India. There was a Christian Endeavor pledge in Urdu, bordered with silhouettes showing life in India. Boys of the Senior society of Sholinghur, North Arcot, had sent a hand-painted pledge in the Tamil language; the Welsh Mission High School for Girls at Shillong, Assam, had sent an artistically lettered pledge in both the Khasi language and in English.

Vere Abbey, consecrated and efficient Christian Endeavor Secretary for India, had sent the garland of everlasting, close-scented blossoms with which the Leper Asylum Christian Endeavor Society of the Tamil Union had honored him. This garland and the printed account of its presentation—and that of a silver tray—to Vere Abbey and his wife brought these old friends very close. We remembered a night in another convention hall, in Berlin   .

In one of the exhibit booths, pigs were being passed out for use—fat little metal pigs with slots in their backs, into which money for the American Mission to Lepers could be inserted. The exhibit of this mission thrilled you and tugged at your heart. Who could see unmoved the pictures of the changes the mission has made in the lives of the world's most unfortunate people? Who could hear, without shame, of the Siamese lepers who were asked to pray for the leper colony at Carville, Louisiana, and who said, "Couldn't we pray better if we gave something?" They each had ten cents a week—their total wealth. They sent to Louisiana forty-one dollars.

No wonder Ohio Christian Endeavorers are glad to support this Mission to Lepers and that other Endeavorers took home many little pigs—and the story of Wilbur and Pete, the first pig—so that they could pray better as they gave.

The Quiet Hour might have been described in leaflets. Instead, it was suggested vividly by a very charming little bedroom, a scene of utter restfulness, in which, on a table by an easy chair, an open Bible and other books for meditation reading were ready for use.

Special Guest at the Opening Session

Rear Admiral Richard Evelyn Byrd
U. S. N., Retired

The Opening Session

Long before the appointed time the eager crowd of delegates had filled the big, cool auditorium. State delegations assembled in their designated sections just long enough to sing a State song, then marched, singing and cheering, up and down the aisles.

"This is a really youthful convention!" an observer would have thought. "Here the spirit of joyous anticipation is bubbling over in laughter and song! Will these young people ever become serious?"

The simplicity of modern architecture at its best made the auditorium an admirable setting. The walls are dark blue and dull silver, and the same color framed the stage, hidden at first by the soft folds of a blue velvet curtain. Just in front of the curtain, on the left side of the stage, stood a great white cross bearing in golden letters the Convention theme, "Christ for the Crisis."

In the excitement of the preliminary hour of songs and greetings, few noticed that just before seven-thirty the chairs on a narrow platform in front of the blue curtain suddenly disappeared. The fact that the platform on which they stood had been lowered to the level of the floor below was concealed by a low curtain hung from just above the press tables to the floor.

But suddenly, a signal brought the delegates to their feet. The songs stopped and there was a moment of wondering silence during which the movable platform rose to a position level with the stage.

Then the silence was shattered by the thunderous clapping of hands. For there on that platform were Christian Endeavor's best-loved leaders! There were President and Mrs. Poling and Vice-Presidents Foulkes and Holmes. There were Carroll Wright and Stanley Vandersall. There were Homer Rodeheaver and his trombone. There were denominational youth leaders. There, for the thrilling of thousands of first-time delegates, was little Mrs. Francis E. Clark herself, smiling with joy! There, quiet and dignified in white linen, was Rear Admiral Richard Evelyn Byrd!

As the applause continued the blue velvet curtains parted to reveal the choir, on tiers of seats that filled the great stage. Above the highest tier of choristers hung the American flag and the Christian flag and a Neon sign that twinkled, "Welcome, C.E.!"

Silence, then, while the auditorium lights were dimmed and only the lighted cross gleamed white and gold in the darkness, and the voices of the choir rang through the stillness,

> In the Cross of Christ I glory,
>   Towering o'er the wrecks of time.
> All the light of sacred story
>   Gathers 'round its head sublime.

The lights shone again and the great audience (*who* asked if these youth could ever be serious?) sat down quietly. Dr. Poling spoke clearly: "I declare the Thirty-sixth International Convention of Christian Endeavor in order!"

Who among those assembled thousands will forget those first moments of the Convention?

Mr. Homer Rodeheaver, giving the audience his inimitable smile, introduced the conductors of the choir, Mr. John B. Klaasse and Mr. Frank B. Goodwin, and then himself led the convention in singing. We sang "All Hail the Power of Jesus' Name," and Mr. Rodeheaver prayed for God's blessing on the gathering. We sang "America the Beautiful," and the chorus "We Choose Christ," reminiscent of the 1935 Philadelphia Convention, and the new theme-chorus, "Christ for the Crisis."

The brief worship service, "The Prophet's Doom and Hope," especially prepared for the convention by Dr. Harry Thomas Stock, was led by the Rev. Lester C. Doerr, Associate Chairman of the Grand Rapids Convention Committee.

"Mother Endeavor" Clark, called by Dr. Poling "eighty-six years young," then spoke to the Convention. Said she:

"I am glad to be with you and to feel that we are all here because we want to do whatsoever our Lord would have us do and because we are pledged to serve Him as long as our lives shall last. May God bless us every one and grant that we may serve Him as long as we shall live!"

Mr. Henry W. Walstrom, City Commissioner, welcomed the Convention to Grand Rapids with the assurance that the delegates had entered "a city of homes, of churches, of religion, of clean living, of health, of parks and playgrounds, of education and schools, and a sincere desire to contribute and share whatever it has to help you to make this Convention a tremendous success."

"Christian Endeavor was born in the church," said Rev. John H. Meengs, President of the Grand Rapids Ministerial Association, on behalf of the city's churches. "It is fitting that your welcome should come from the churches. I hope for you the inspiration of a mountain-top experience and the development of new loyalties to Christ. Above all I pray that Christian youth will be challenged to meet the crisis."

Dr. William Hiram Foulkes, newly elected Moderator of the Presbyterian General Assembly, a Vice-President of the International Society of Christian Endeavor, was introduced to the Convention. He was presented with a gift from the Board of Trustees of the International Society of Christian Endeavor (a Telechron) and in expressing his appreciation of the gift, whimsically called himself "Dr. Poling's only 'vice.' " He added that he had come with heart and head and hands to serve the Convention.

The Nation Listened In

The Convention choir sang beautifully and then the Convention was "on the air" for a nation-wide broadcast. To begin the broadcast the delegates sang the first stanza of "America," one stanza of "Faith of Our Fathers," and "Christ for the Crisis."

Dr. Poling then read a message from the mother of Admiral Byrd, who telegraphed:

"It is one of the greatest disappointments of my life that I cannot be with you tonight. I believe this citation is the most wonderful thing ever done for my son."

Mr. Howard D. Cole, President of the Oregon Christian Endeavor Union, moved that a telegram be sent in reply to the greeting from President Roosevelt. The president's message was read by Dr. William Hiram Foulkes, Vice-President of the International Society.

Mrs. Clark, presented to the radio audience, said:

"I am very grateful for this friendly greeting and feel that you are all working together for the Kingdom of God and that God has given to each one of us some little share in the work for Christ and the Church."

Dr. Poling then presented to Admiral Richard Evelyn Byrd a Scroll of Achievement, the International Youth's Distinguished Service Citation. Said Dr. Poling:

It is now my privilege and honor, on behalf of the International Society of Christian Endeavor and of the World's Christian Endeavor Union, to confer on Rear Admiral Richard Evelyn Byrd International Youth's Distinguished Service Citation.

Admiral Byrd, you are youth's hero tale of a generation—courage and faith, genius for organization, and contributions to scientific achievement, idealism and devotion to a great cause, unite in you to produce one of the preeminent personalities of our time.

You have received world recognition and the honors of the most distinguished societies in many fields, but here and now you are to receive one award that is perhaps unique—International Youth's Distinguished Service Citation. Before these delegates of all the states and provinces of North America, with notable representatives present from foreign lands, and with the world listening in, you are recognized, not only for your scientific achievements but particularly because of your dedication to and leadership in the cause of world peace.

Your story, sir, is an epic tale. It was during your long, six-months vigil at Advance Base, the world's southernmost outpost, that you reached your high resolve to dedicate your life to peace. Too sick to eat, your vitality reduced to the point of utter exhaustion, you steadfastly adhered to your iron code. Deliberately you chose to die rather than endanger your men.

Stricken by poisonous fumes, helpless in your tiny shack, in the utter solitude of the Antarctic night, your body chilled but your brain afire, your mind turned to the contemplation of human relations. Surely God spoke then to your soul. Now we know that you reached the conviction that the greatest of all human follies is war, and that you made the inviolable decision that if by miracle you survived your ordeal, you would devote what remained of your life and your powers to war's abolition.

It is upon you as Admiral Richard Evelyn Byrd certainly, but upon you as "Dick Byrd, Gallant Gentleman" equally, that international youth through Christian Endeavor, with its more than four million members in eighty-six nations, confers now this citation.

God bless you, sir, and may you have increasing good success.

Address of Admiral Byrd

Admiral Byrd modestly accepted the Scroll of Achievement and then gave the address of the evening, on peace. The full text follows.

These thousands of young people make the most moving scene I have ever witnessed. There would be no need to speak of peace if all the people of the world lived up to the standards set by you.

I would rather not see you work for peace unless you do so in a practical way, with your feet on the ground. If you give your backing to an impractical peace plan you are likely to do more harm than good. To be well-meaning is not enough. We all know what is paved with good intentions!

It is not always easy to keep your feet on the ground or to be free of emotions where national problems are concerned, and it is much harder to do so with international problems.

In recent years democracies have been up for trial, on the defensive and possibly slowly passing from the earth unless the citizens of democracies take more interest in the affairs of their governments. The lazy man's government is the dictatorship which, at the cost of liberty, relieves the citizen of the necessity of thinking for himself.

We can't be lazy if we expect to keep what we have. The State Department, almost more than any other branch of our government, needs your intelligent interest and backing. The transcendently important work of the Secretary of State is made much more difficult for him by the tremendous lack of knowledge in this country of the problems connected with our relations with other nations. Mr. Hull is very wise, able and tolerant, and no one desires peace any more than he does. But his position requires him, above all things, to face solid facts. Some of his problems he can publicize only after they are solved, and in other cases his good work, for diplomatic reasons, must forever remain unknown and uncredited. Half-baked, emotional peace propaganda only adds to his burdens.

If you could see behind the scenes of our State Department, you would find that they constantly face difficult situations, at times so delicate in nature that it takes very little to upset the apple cart.

I would like to see some wealthy citizen establish an unofficial, nonpartisan, non-political, information bureau designed to make available to every one desiring them the solid facts (that of course are not confidential) of our international difficulties. Such a bureau could, I believe, be a big help in steering many peace organizations in the right direction.

I mention "solid facts" because in order to bring about a world as we would like it to be, it is imperative that we face the world of today as it is.

Here is an example of what I mean by facing facts: The peace-at-any-price groups in the larger democratic countries have been so very active that the militaristic and intensely nationalistic countries have come to have the mistaken belief that democracies are approaching the state of peace-at-any-price nations.

The result is natural and in fact inevitable. Most militaristic nations take

STANLEY B. VANDERSALL
Associate Secretary

CARROLL M. WRIGHT
*Treasurer and Financial
Secretary*

ARTHUR J. STANLEY
Associate President

PAUL C. BROWN
General Representative

ROBERT S. NANCE
Extension Secretary

Officers of the International Society

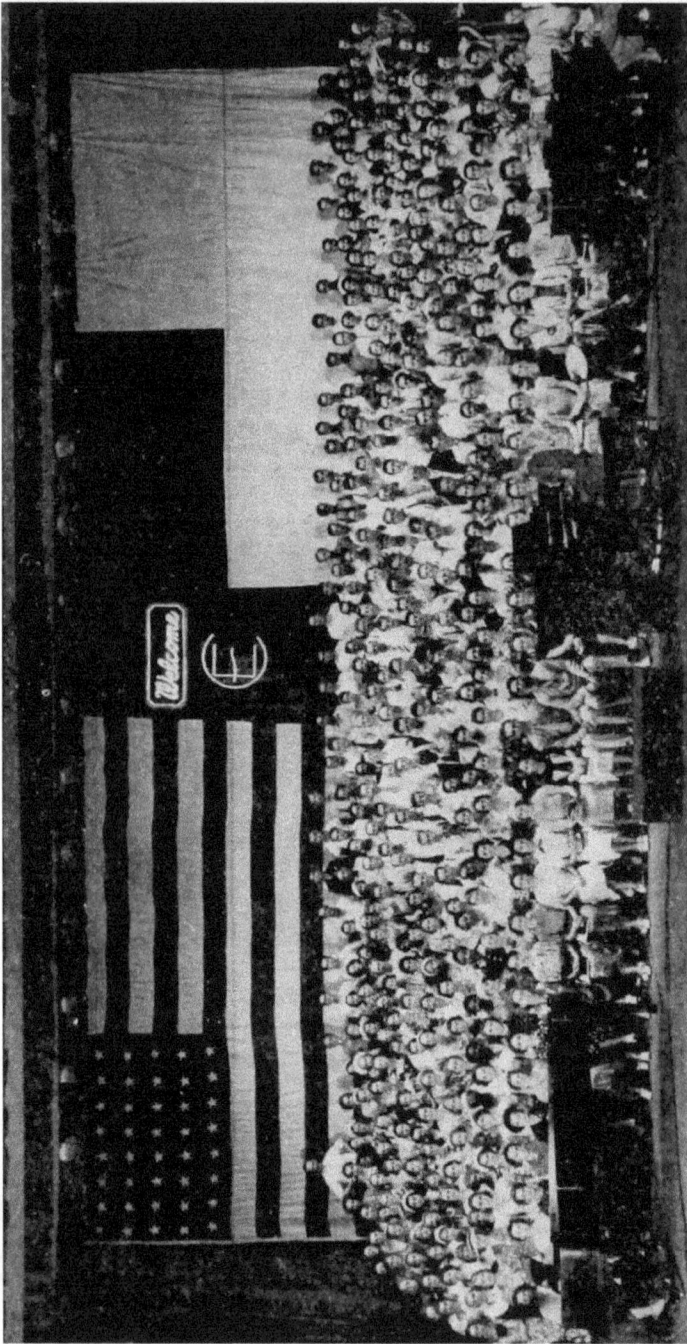

"The Curtains Parted to Reveal the Choir"

full advantage of the situation and proceed to tear up treaties and break international law wherever it suits them to do so, and to take by force, if they can, what they think they need. With cold-blooded calculation, these nations have counted upon the love of peace in democracies to save them from punishment for their wrong doing. They will continue to go as far as they can until some kind of force (I hope it won't have to be the force of war) stops them. Recognizing only force, these autocratic governments lose much respect for peace loving democracies. Our friendliness they mistake for softness. That is the wherefore of England's great rearmament program.

In fairness, I want to point out that some of these militaristic nations are the "have nots" in the family of nations. They lack territory or vital raw material necessary, they think, for their national life. Other nations, they claim, have long ago taken or procured what they need and now don't want the "have not" nations to do the same.

Why, they argue, should they be kept from getting what they need? At least that argument is human, and the family of nations should pay more attention than they do towards making it possible for them to get what they consider necessary for their national life.

It is human for a citizen in a land of plenty to be dissatisfied when he lacks the necessities of a normal life. It is human for a nation in a world of plenty to be dissatisfied when it lacks the necessities for its national existence. I say this in justice to the militaristic nations and not in condonement of their methods. The "have nots," whether they are individuals or nations, will always be belligerent if they cannot procure necessities by peaceful means.

To get back to my line of thought. Democracies are not peace-at-any-price nations—not by a great deal—and they resent more than has appeared on the surface the pugnaciousness and the lawlessness of aggressor nations Further, they believe that there are some things worse than a threatened war—namely, a bigger or a more dangerous war; or the complete loss of democracy and so liberty from the face of the earth.

To sum up and admit the truth. Acquisitive nations, like acquisitive men, not held in leash by law, have a tendency to bully the weak and take what they need, respecting only power. It is, therefore, dangerous to peace for a nation to lose prestige by giving the appearance of weakness. It is high time for democracies to bring to the surface that firmness and strength of character which they really possess.

I hope that the above example will show you what I mean by keeping your feet on the ground. The peace-at-any-price group have in this case, by a refusal to face the facts of life, defeated their purpose.

Now, most peace-at-any-price citizens are sincere and honest. For example, I respect and admire the Quakers. It is part of their religion to refuse to fight. They have, I believe, a part to play in the great scheme of things. I am glad that they are keeping the light burning. There are other such groups that are sincere and I believe also have their place in the scheme of things.

On the other hand, several peace-at-any-price groups are working for the complete disarmament of this nation as a means of destroying our democratic form of government.

Because I have asked you to keep your feet on the ground doesn't mean that I am asking you to relinquish any of your ideals. But is it not necessary to face the world as it is in order to bring to pass a world as you would like it to be?

Cling to your ideals. Don't permit the faults of human nature to destroy them, for the ideals of youth will some day be justified.

And now that I have talked so much about your keeping your feet on the ground I guess it is up to me to try to give you some solid facts about peace.

First, and I believe very important for you to comprehend, is that rapid transportation and instant communication have made us an integral part of the world. Time and space no longer keep nations apart. Isolation is no longer possible. We are deeply involved with other nations in finance, in trade, in science and in culture

This nation cannot escape its responsibility as a member of the family of nations, as a part of the human race.

If there is a general foreign war that, by some near miracle we are not drawn into, we would, as certainly as night follows the day, suffer the economic depression, the political upheavals, and the crash of civilization that would inevitably result.

The only way to keep this nation from suffering the terrible consequences of foreign war is to keep other great nations from fighting.

It is our duty to ourselves, therefore, as well as to the rest of the world, to do everything humanly possible to prevent a foreign war, by taking such action as that of demanding in time of crisis that conciliation and arbitration be substituted for war.

Second, there is a defeatist attitude regarding peace that is assumed by millions of citizens throughout the world, greatly retarding the cause of a better international organization. This group claims that the task of bringing about peace is an impossible one and that, therefore, nothing should be done about the matter. There are many reasons why this is a very bad attitude to assume. Of course, if we are to keep our feet on the ground, we must admit that it may take a very long time to achieve peace. But working honestly for it is one of the most salutary things that can happen to the world, because in the process of working for peace nations must do a thousand things, big and little, national and international, that should have been done long ago and which are vitally important to the well-being of our nation. One thing, for example, is that people will have to be taught that the most efficient thing to do within a nation and without, is for groups of citizens to show a friendly consideration of and co-operation with other groups. It is thus that the well-being of the family units throughout the world can best be served. In order to show consideration for others, a knowledge of their problems is necessary, and accurate knowledge in the vast majority of cases, makes for tolerance and understanding.

We will have to learn the value to the individual, to the group, and to the nation, of self-restraint, and so I want to say with emphasis that a man can have no better ideal, no better way to fit himself into the great scheme of things, than that of working for the ideal of peace. His work, if intelligently applied, will be beneficial to the world entirely aside from the goal to be achieved. Don't let the defeatist group deter you from working for peace. A sincere interest in this great cause will give you an anchor to windward in this storm-tossed world.

This is the second solid fact I have to give you regarding peace.

Third, there is another group that I have called the adamant group. The members of this group are passionately devoted to the cause of peace, but follow very rigidly some peace formulae. They are uncompromising, unbending, as immovable as a mountain. The men and women in this group are fine citizens as a rule. The adamantist, being intolerant of the views of others, is antagonistic to those whose doctrines differ from his, and so we witness some of the peace forces fighting among themselves. We have such doctrinaires in every branch of activity. It is not confined to the peace worker. Don't become an adamantist.

Fourth. There is a *fight instinct* that lies deep in most of us. That fight urge comes to the surface when the war clouds gather and feet are heard marching to the drums and martial music. Emotion replaces reason. We must take into account this war fever if we are to have an antidote for it to prevent emotion from replacing calm reason. Education as to the truth of war is the serum to use.

Fifth. Entirely aside from the question of peace, it is of transcendent importance to bring to pass a far better world organization than exists. Isolation, as I have pointed out, being impossible (and most undesirable if it were possible), we must have very numerous and often very complicated dealings with our fellow nations. The social, cultural, and scientific contacts go along fairly smoothly, though there are not enough of them. Our economic dealings, however, are at the present stage of international co-operation, sources of dangerous irritation. The less nations meet for conciliation, the more the irritation and danger from the economic and financial complications.

Business men could not carry on business in an efficient and friendly way if they did not get together to discuss their mutual and individual problems. No more can nations have an efficient international organization if they refuse to form the habit of meeting sufficiently often—in time of peace at the table of discussion and in time of crisis at the table of arbitration. What is so often lost sight of is that an efficient international organization would do very much for the internal well-being of nations and bring about longer and longer periods of peace.

This nation has considered it unwise to join the League of Nations as a means of international discussion and conciliation. But some kind of international machinery is necessary. This country should therefore, encourage the formation of a suitable association of nations that will not have the, to some, objectionable features of the League.

Sixth. There is no one formula (aside from the one Christ gave us, which we refuse to follow) that will, if adhered to, achieve peace. It must be striven for, as I have said, on a thousand fronts. Man's reactions are greatly influenced by his knowledge and intelligence, and his reactions are under control only insofar as he exercises self-restraint. Nine hundred of the fronts, therefore, are along the line of education and self-discipline. There is no easy or short road to peace. The individual must be taught where he fits into his nation and into a world greatly shrunk by the conquering of space and the removal of time as bars to communication.

To sum up, Europeans, though on the other side of the ocean, are, in a sense, our neighbors. They can talk to us over the radio. When television comes we can see them as well as hear them. We buy from and sell to them We profit by their scientific discoveries and cultural advancement. When an economic collapse strikes them we suffer with them. The 1914-18 struggle showed that a great war affects the whole world; even the non-combatants suffered. The 1929 economic collapse proved that a great depression also affects the whole world If other nations suffer morally or spiritually we inevitably feel the effect. We are bound together as members of the human race so that the well-being of a nation is affected by the well-being of another nation. The great thing, therefore, that people of the world must learn, which must be applied among groups within nations and among nations within the great family of nations, can be expressed in one magnificent word, "Co-operation."

Is not that in a nutshell what Christ taught two thousand years ago? It has long been our religion and it has now become a necessity for the survival of our new civilization, the mark of which is the great interdependence of human relationship among individuals of nations and among nations in the family of nations.

Admiral Byrd's address was given thoughtful attention and enthusiastically applauded. The Convention sang the last stanza of "America" and the broadcast was concluded.

Following the broadcast Dr. Poling explained that Admiral Byrd was serving as Chairman for the Emergency Peace Campaign, in which all the peace organizations are working together.

Dr. Stanley B. Vandersall, Associate Secretary of the International Society of Christian Endeavor, was introduced to the convention and spoke on "Christian Endeavor's Relations with Other Organizations." Said Dr. Vandersall:

Mr. Chairman, Mother Clark, Fellow Endeavorers all:

From the beginning of Christian Endeavor more than fifty years ago, there has been a natural and a pleasant connection with the denominations which it came to serve. When, in the genius of the society, there came to be conferences and conventions calling together enthusiastic Christian Endeavor leaders from many denominations, the organization began to make history in the field of co-operative enterprises. As societies increased in number and power, the stronger denominations named secretaries of Christian Endeavor work. Later they established departments of young people's activities; and in our day there exist in most of the denominations strong and active boards of Christian education embracing all phases of young people's work. Christian Endeavor continues to flourish as a strong evangelical training organization in more than fifty denominations in North America. But it also is rightly classified as a great interdenominational force in the field of youth.

In line with its spirit and principle, Christian Endeavor has readily allied itself with emphases, organizations, and movements whenever and wherever it could serve the cause of youth. It was foremost in promoting missionary activity among young people. It took a prominent lead in citizenship declarations—indeed, before many of the individual denominations did so. It developed personal devotions through the department of the Quiet Hour, and personal stewardship through the department of the Tenth Legion. Its conventions through several decades have carried the standards of unity and of co-operation.

The International Society has recognized that its leadership must come from the denominations, and therefore it has depended on bishops, moderators, presidents, pastors, department secretaries, leaders of young people, and many others prominent in church life to assume places of leadership in the interdenominational movement. In co-operative enterprises, in education, missions, citizenship, and many other worthy causes, Christian Endeavor finds a natural place. The International Society maintains friendly relationships with the International Council of Religious Education and its several divisions in the field of youth. It has heartily co-operated in the United Christian Youth Movement since its inception three years ago. It enthusiastically supports and has participation in interdenominational projects for peace, for citizenship, for evangelism, and for other worthy sections of the Christian enterprise.

The secretaries and other leaders of the International Society are thus brought into direct and frequent contact with other leaders in the field of youth. I have the privilege, and a distinct one it is, to present to the President, so that he in turn may present to the audience, a number of the leaders in young people's work in the great evangelical denominations of our country. These friendly and constructive supporters of Christian Endeavor and the things which we do together are a fine asset to this Convention, and it is a pleasure to give them acclaim.

Dr. Vandersall then presented to Dr. Poling, who in turn presented them to the Convention, the following denominational directors of young people's work:

James W. Eichelberger, Director of Christian Education, A.M.E. Zion Church.

Frank D. Getty, Director of Young People's Work, Presbyterian Church, U. S. A.

GEORGE VELDMAN
*General Chairman of the Grand Rapids
Convention Committee*

Richard A. Hoiland, Director of Young People's Work, American Baptist Publication Society.

Myron T. Hopper, Director of Young People's Work, Disciples of Christ.

J. Gordon Howard, Director of Young People's Work, United Brethren in Christ.

S. S. Moris, Secretary of Christian Endeavor, A.M.E. Church.

Herbert L. Minard, Editor, *The Front Rank.*

Raymond M. Veh, Editor, *The Evangelical Crusader.*

Martin L. Harvey, Director of Young People's Work, A.M.E. Zion Church.

Buford S. Gordon, Editor of Young People's Literature, A.M.E. Zion Church.

W. E. Peffley, Editor of Sunday School and Young People's Literature, The Evangelical Church.

Harry Thomas Stock, Secretary of Student and Young People's Work, Congregational Education Society.

Mr. Rodeheaver made a brief but telling appeal for funds for the world-wide work of Christian Endeavor and the offering was received by the corps of lovely young women ushers. In neat, red-piped white linen dresses and red "halos," these ushers made a most attractive picture as they moved quietly about the auditorium.

During the offering interval Mr. Rodeheaver played "The Holy City" on the trombone, after which the choir sang the new song, "Follow, I Will Follow Thee," by Howard Brown, General Secretary for California.

Mr. Carroll M. Wright, Treasurer and Financial Secretary of the International Society of Christian Endeavor, was introduced by Dr. Poling. Mr. Wright said:

The International Society of Christian Endeavor has always been a clearing house for plans and programs. Its work is of no avail without the activity of the State unions, and the co-operation of the State workers who are on the firing line. who can give direct help to the local churches. So I want you to know those splendid men and women, our State field secretaries.

Mr. Wright then presented to Dr. Poling, who in turn presented them to the audience, the following men and women:

Ernest S. Marks, Michigan	Dr. Paul C. Brown, California
Russell J. Blair, Massachusetts	Warren G. Hoopes, Pennsylvania
Mrs. Dorothy Mackenzie, New Hampshire	Fred L. Mintel, New Jersey
Mary E. Jackson, West Virginia	Earle W. Gates, New York
Elizabeth Cooper. Nebraska	Margaret Reynolds, Missouri
Vernon L. Phillips, Connecticut	Lawrence W. Bash. Iowa
J. E. Abnett, Kentucky	Chester Rutledge, Washington
George R. Sweet, Indiana	Harvey N. Marks, Colorado
George H. Wilson, Southern States	Robert S. Nance, Kansas
Aldis L. Webb, Texas	

The first evening's session, so crammed with interest and inspiration, was closed with a prayer and benediction by Dr. Raymond M. Veh, Editor of *The Evangelical Crusader*.

Dimmed lights and a moment of silence—then the great audience arose. The first session was over. The Convention had begun gloriously!

III

Each Day Brings Its Gifts

"May every morning seem to say,
'There's something happy on the way,
And God sends love to you!'"

THIS wish was answered completely in those never-to-be-for-gotten days in Grand Rapids. Each day resembled all the others in that each day was joyous and friendly and thought-provoking, yet each day had a definite individuality of its own.

Thursday

Thursday was a day of eager anticipation—anticipation realized in the glorious opening session Thursday evening. "Even if this were all, even if I had to leave tonight, I should be thankful that I had been here!" one delegate declared after the first session closed. And a mother and two daughters in Brooklyn, New York, who heard the broadcast of part of the opening session, telegraphed to Dr. Poling that they had not thought of attending the Convention, but that they were impelled, by their interest in the broadcast, to make new plans and to leave at once for Grand Rapids.

Admiral Byrd's address excited comment in many places far from the Convention Auditorium. After the broadcast of his address on peace he received ninety telegrams and two cablegrams from foreign countries expressing approval of what he had said.

Friday

Friday was a day of self-examination. The theme for the day, "Personal Christian Living," suggested the first phase of the general theme of the Educational Conferences, "Christian Youth Building a New World."

Dr. William Hiram Foulkes, in his Quiet Hour talk, emphasized the importance of an increasing consciousness of God in our own lives and of changing those lives through His grace. Dr. Harry Thomas Stock, in the Introductory Conference Session, urged that we discover how a Christian should be different from non-Christians. In the conferences there was a serious attempt to answer this question.

The general Convention session of the morning was presided over by Mr. Norman Klauder of Philadelphia, a member of the

Board of Trustees. A young man of unusually attractive personality, earnest, sincere and well-poised, was the speaker—Mr. Lanson Granger, President of the National Pilgrim Fellowship, youth division of the Congregational and Christian Churches. Mr. Granger spoke eloquently on the subject, "Youth Taking Christ Seriously."

At this session Mr. George Southwell showed pictures taken at the Mission for Lepers in the Belgian Congo. Mr. Southwell announced the raising of $400 by the Endeavorers of Ohio to build a schoolhouse for the mission. This schoolhouse will be called the Poling-Massman School, in honor of Dr. Poling and Mr. Glen Massman, Christian Endeavor Field Secretary for Ohio.

Miss Helen L. Lyon of Washington, D. C., presided at the Young People's Radio Conference, during which Dr. Poling spoke on the subject, "Life's Ultimatum—Fix It or Face It!" After his brief radio address Dr. Poling answered questions which had been put to him by delegates at the Convention. (See Chapter VII.)

Friday afternoon was devoted to the separate meetings of the various denominations. These meetings, for fellowship, for the introduction of denominational leaders to delegates from all parts of the country, and for discussion of questions relating to the denominational programs and interdenominational relationships, were enthusiastically attended. Some of the denominations had planned sightseeing trips through Grand Rapids after their meeting; others held banquets at the dinner hour and ended just in time for the delegates to attend the evening session of the Convention.

Friday Evening

Again the great auditorium was filled with an eager throng of delegates. Again the choir of five hundred voices delighted the audience. "In the Cross of Christ I Glory," and "Open Their Eyes," an anthem by McFarland, were two of the selections which proved the excellence of the singers' voices and the thoroughness of their training. Again Mr. Homer Rodeheaver led the delegates in singing with such joyous expression that many felt, "I never knew what singing could be, until now!"

Miss Donna Chappell of Memphis, Missouri, and Mr. Ronald Keeler of Bloomsburg, Pennsylvania, were introduced to the convention by Dr. Poling. These young people were awarded a trip to the Convention with all expenses paid by *The Lookout*, a magazine of Christian education of which Mr. Guy P. Leavitt is the editor. The award to these young people was made on the basis of their outstanding usefulness to their own local churches.

Then one of the high-lights of the Convention—Dr. Poling's

presidential address, "Christ for the Crisis!" Here was the story of Christian Endeavor's achievement the world around; here was a picture of present-day youth and its needs; here was an urgent description of our civilization's present crisis. And here was the answer to all problems: "Christ for the Crisis!" (For a complete report of this address see Chapter VI.)

Saturday

Good fellowship was the keynote of Saturday. All days promoted good fellowship, yet Saturday offered unusual opportunities for its expression. Dr. John R. Mulder in the Quiet Hour emphasized fellowship with Jesus. In the introductory Conference session Dr. Stock urged the delegates to think of the problems and the responsibilities of our fellowship in the church. The conference theme for the day was "Building through the Church."

Two friends representing other organizational relationships spoke to the delegates at the general Convention session following the conferences. Rev. Ivan M. Gould, Associate Director of Young People's Work of the International Council of Religious Education, was introduced by the presiding officer, Mr. Albert Arend of Spokane, Washington.

Mr. Gould described the united youth movement, "Christian Youth Building a New World." Christian Endeavor is co-operating in this movement.

A present activity of this youth movement is that of giving relief to the children of Spain, helping to clothe and feed and house the refugee children of *all* factions. This practical demonstration of the will to world peace was described by Miss Emily Parker, Young People's Work Director for the Society of Friends. Miss Parker will go to Spain in the near future as the direct representative of the young people in the United States. She will work through the American Friends Service Committee. Miss Parker appealed for co-operation in the raising of funds to help carry on this most urgent and vital work.

Mr. Harry N. Holmes presided over the Young People's Radio Conference, during which Dr. Poling spoke on the subject, "Youth Marches."

Youth marched, not to the tragic consequences Dr. Poling described in his radio address, but for the glory of God, in the great Christian Endeavor parade on Saturday afternoon. All Grand Rapids came to view the parade and generously applauded it. It is fully described in Chapter X.

Six o'clock was the time set for the official Convention Banquet, Saturday evening, but at five-thirty guests overflowed from the banquet hall into three other large dining rooms. Here was an outstanding opportunity for fellowship!

So was the evening session, in which the people of Grand Rapids gave a pageant which, in the words of Dr. Poling, "left an indelible impression."

Saturday was surely a day of good fellowship.

Sunday

In any International Christian Endeavor Convention, Sunday is a Day of Reconsecration. So it was in Grand Rapids. From the beginning of the early morning communion service to the benediction Sunday night there was a keen awareness of the presence of God. No one who took part in it will ever forget the quiet beauty of the communion service, in which thousands of young people kept the covenant established by Jesus at His Last Supper.

Dr. William Hiram Foulkes, Moderator of the General Assembly of the Presbyterian Church in the U. S. A., directed the service, assisted by Rev. John H. Meengs and a group of Grand Rapids ministers and elders. Many delegates commented on the quick and orderly fashion in which the whole vast congregation was served. There was no slightest defect to mar an atmosphere of perfect reverence.

Convention speakers and leaders filled the pulpits of Grand Rapids and neighboring communities, and delegates attended the churches of their choice. To the people of Grand Rapids was thus carried the spirit of the Convention. They most cordially welcomed the visitors into their churches as they had already welcomed many into their homes.

Most delegates wished, on Sunday afternoon, that they were triplets at the least! For simultaneous meetings offered a variety of appealing programs.

The Auditorium Meeting

In the main Auditorium Miss Helen L. Lyon presided over a meeting of exceptional interest. Following one of Mr. Rodeheaver's inimitable services of song, Dr. Norma P. Dunning, one of the most radiant leaders in the Convention, spoke about her work in South Bombay, India. Dr. Dunning did not give a stereotyped appeal for missions; rather, she transported her audience to a far country where she made them familiar with people who are desperately in need of medical help and everlastingly grateful for that help and for the story of the love of Christ which made that help possible.

There was the man who had been healed in the mission hospital and who wanted to thank the missionaries in a very practical way. Once every year he walked fourteen miles to bring them the one rupee which he could so ill afford to give. One year, because of trouble at home, he missed coming; the next year he very carefully brought *two* rupees. (A rupee is about thirty cents in American money.)

Dr. Dunning contradicted the idea sometimes advanced by those who do not believe in missionary work, that the people of India accept the medical help but not the Christian religion. She told of sick men eagerly reading the Bible through the night, pleading, "I must learn this before I die." She told of a man explaining that the religion of the Hindus and Buddhism are beautiful and colorful but they are dry and dead. Only the religion of Jesus is alive.

It was clearly evident that self-sacrificing Dr. Dunning is a living demonstration to India of the reality of the religion of Jesus.

Following Dr. Dunning's address, Bishop Linwood Westinghouse Kyles of the A.M.E. Zion Church gave a very scholarly address on the subject, "Christ Meeting America's Needs." (See Chapter VI for quotations.)

At this meeting Rev. Gene Stone of Philadelphia and Miss Phyllis Brown of Richmond led in prayer.

Interest Groups

Three interest groups met simultaneously with the meeting in the Auditorium.

Mr. W. Roy Breg led a group in the discussion of "Christian Endeavor and the Liquor Traffic." In this discussion helpful facts were contributed by Mr. Homer Rodeheaver and Rev. Robert S. Nance, who told how young people had worked to secure the vote of the people of Kansas for a dry state. Mr. Breg gave practical suggestions about the way the educational movement, Allied Youth, is helping young people all over the country to face the facts about liquor choices and the human cost of drink and to take constructive action.

Mrs. Daniel A. Poling led another large and thoughtful group in a discussion of "Preparation for Marriage." Mrs. Poling stressed the importance of intelligent preparation and the qualities of character which make successful marriage possible. Mr. Reuel B. Wolford of Pennsylvania presided at this meeting.

In a third meeting "Missionary Action Today" was discussed under the able leadership of Miss Ruth Seabury. Delegates were helped to see how the missionary program meets conditions in foreign countries today.

Sunday Evening

For a great many Endeavorers the Sunday evening meeting was the very best part of the entire Convention. It was not a peak from which the remainder of the Convention fell away, but rather the entrance to a spiritual plateau, a new high level on which the Convention would live.

Dr. John A. Dykstra of the Central Reformed Church, Grand Rapids, led the worship service. Mr. Rodeheaver sang "In the Secret of His Presence." The choir again sent its message of melodious beauty to the delegates' hearts. Mr. Ernest R. Bryan, Superintendent of Christian Endeavor's World Peace Fellowship, appealed to the delegates to enroll in this Fellowship. There was a gratifying, immediate response to this call.

Then—that part of the Convention program which so many Endeavorers had eagerly awaited—the address of Dr. Louis H. Evans, minister of the Third Presbyterian Church of Pittsburgh, Pennsylvania. Anticipation was not disappointed. Dr. Evans' message was even more eloquent, more heart-searching than convention sessions usually provide. As he spoke on "The Glory of the Crisis," as he called to youth to dare to live dangerously, to follow the hard way of Christ, the glorious Commander, the great audience sat tense and still. Here was a man who knew the hopes and dreams of youth, challenging youth to the almost impossible. Here was a man whom youth heard gladly and to whose call they were ready to respond.

They did respond when a little later Dr. Poling gave them the opportunity. Scores of them rose and came to the platform making their first public confession of Jesus as Saviour and Lord. Scores who were already active members of the Christian church came to signify their intention to enter full-time Christian service. Who knows how many others, who did not stand before the Convention, still made a quiet dedication of their hearts and lives to "the glorious Commander"? Who knows what good purposes were strengthened, what fears overcome?

It was indeed a night of sacred reconsecration.

Monday

Monday could be called the Day of Determination. Inspired by all that had gone before, stirred to new purpose by the Sunday evening meeting, the delegates faced the problems to be considered on Monday with a new zeal to discover ways of taking action.

There was a more general participation in discussion in the educational conferences, more seriousness in the attention given

THE EXHIBIT OF THE WORLD-WIDE WORK OF CHRISTIAN ENDEAVOR, ASSEMBLED BY THE MISSIONARY DEPARTMENT OF THE MICHIGAN UNION

to the platform speakers. It seemed as if with one accord the entire host of delegates surged forward toward goals which now all could see.

Monday afternoon was set aside particularly for the holding of State conventions and other meetings of delegations. Michigan had a large and enthusiastic crowd in the Convention Auditorium, elected officers, chose Kalamazoo as convention city for 1938, when the fiftieth anniversary of the movement in Michigan will occur, and wound up the celebration by a monster Michigan banquet in the Pantlind Hotel.

Indiana held its annual convention in the Red Room of the Auditorium. Officers were elected, and plans were made for the Golden Jubilee of Christian Endeavor in Indiana in next year's convention at Indianapolis.

Wisconsin enjoyed a delightful luncheon at the Y.W.C.A., with the annual business meeting of the State Union following. The new officers led in the making of plans for the new year.

FRED R. ROY
Adult-Alumni Department

MRS. NINA ROWLAND GANO
Intermediate Department

RALPH R. GILBY
Citizenship and Social Issues Department

ERNEST R. BRYAN
World Peace Department

MISS PHYLLIS G. BROWN
Quiet Hour Department

GENE STONE
Tenth Legion Department

MRS. REBA RICKMAN
Lookout and Extension Department

DR. DARRELL C. CRAIN
Social and Recreational Department

MISS JULIA VANGENDEREN
Missionary and Service Department

The New Department Superintendents
(Two are yet to be chosen)

IV

Pages from a Delegate's Diary

Monday

Phil and Dick and Ruth and I had an early breakfast together. We were late for Quiet Hour on Saturday and we were determined not to let that happen again. Quiet Hour is too good to miss.

Dick didn't have much to say this morning—probably because he has so much to think about. He was one of the young people who last night responded to Dr. Poling's call to give their lives in full-time Christian service. That means changing some of the plans he had made for his life-work, but I'm awfully glad he did it. Dick's a grand person! I—well, never mind that!

Dr. Norman Vincent Peale spoke in Quiet Hour this morning. He asked, "How can God become real to you as an individual?" Then he said: "There can be little progress in Christianizing the world while God is only a theological idea. Many people have never felt aware of Him; they do not know Him as they know a beloved friend. We must make our relationship with Him simpler. A profound philosophical or metaphysical approach is unnecessary. We must be as little children.

"A young man in my congregation came to me for help. He was a collector for a business firm and sometimes when his pockets were filled with the firm's money, he was tempted to gamble. Afterward he became remorseful and wanted to know how to overcome the temptation. I told him that God would help him, and he went away. But he gambled again.

"Then I suggested that he imagine that Jesus was at his side; that at a time of temptation he would try to talk to Jesus; to make Him so real that there would be no doubt of His presence. I asked, 'Will you try it?' The young man said he would.

"A month later he came to see me again. He said, 'What do you mean, imagination? When the temptation came I felt a strong hand grip my own and a voice whisper, "Steady now!" Temptation became insignificant. I know that Jesus was as real as you are just now.'

"This young man became as a little child. He believed an impossible thing and it became true. The heart of a child says, 'Nothing in this world is too good to be true!' "

Dr. Peale told us then that we must surrender our lives, our worries, troubles, fears and temptations. God is not real to us because He is not trusted. Religion is not intellectual belief; it is resting your life on the power of God.

39

He said that we must believe on Him a little harder; that when we believe with heart and soul, He will give strength to overcome. He becomes wonderfully real. We were reminded of the scene in Bernard Shaw's play, "St. Joan," where the French commander asks, "How can we conquer with so few men?" and Joan replies, holding up her sword,

"You see that sword? I found it behind the altar in the church of St. Catherine. This is God's sword! With the sword of God no host is mighty enough to prevail against us!"

"I take the sword of God," said Dr. Peale, "and all my weakness disappears. I beat my way with God's sword against all the difficulties which beset my path. If we believe in God Himself, instead of in a bright idea for an organization, irresistible power comes to us. Say, 'I can do all things through Christ who giveth me the strength.' Say it—and really believe it—and you will be a new creature."

Plenty for me to think about in *that* talk.

*　　*　　*

The introductory conference session was different this morning. Instead of one person to point out questions which might be considered in the first period conferences, when the entire convention, in small alphabetical groups, discusses some aspect of "Christian Youth Building a New World," we had three people.

The theme for today was "A Christian Nation." Mr. W. Roy Breg, Executive Secretary of Allied Youth, suggested some questions about the liquor problem as it affects our nation: (1) Why do young people drink? (2) What are the dangers of drinking? (3) What alternatives to drinking can be suggested? (4) How can youth be given the facts about alcohol and induced to take action?

Mr. Breg gave us some points about Allied Youth. I wonder if we could start an Allied Youth Post in our high school? Phil and I could try.

Catherine Miller Balm opened up the subject of race prejudice. She was Director of Young People's Work for the Reformed Church for twelve years. Now she writes books. I copied what she said, because if there is one subject our society needs to tackle soon it is that of race prejudice. Some of our members are terribly biased against people of other races. Well, so was I until I went to a summer conference, and learned to think differently. I went to Mrs. Balm and asked her for a copy of her speech. This is what she gave me:

Recently a man wrote to a magazine to express his disapproval of its policy of recognizing achievement no matter to what race or nation the one honored might belong. He gave as the reason for his attitude, "*I* am a true-blue American and a white Christian!"

Here is an ugly sample of pride, of national and racial exclusiveness, which is not the peculiar possession of white Americans, as you soon discover when *you* are the foreigner in another country. This pride, this exclusiveness, is common enough, but can you be truly Christian and possess it?

We agreed on Friday that a Christian should be demonstrably different from non-Christians. Can you choose Christ and despise people of other races, other colors? Or dare you be different—perhaps queerly, outrageously different—in the eyes of your fellow citizens, and prove that you are completely without prejudice, and that you will not tolerate the continuance of existing discrimination and injustice?

Overcoming prejudice, breaking down barriers between races and nations, isn't easy. You can't do it by singing "In Christ There Is No East or West," or by flowery speeches about the brotherhood of man. How can you do it?

You might begin by examining the barriers. Of what are they built? Is there any justification for considering your race superior, others inferior? What have other races and nations achieved? What are they capable of achieving, granted the same opportunities you have enjoyed? Do nations and races differ in vital matters of character and conduct, or in trivial matters of custom—what they wear, what they eat for breakfast? Do you call an Italian a "Wop" because he reeks of garlic? The Chinese says of *you*, "Phew! The foreign devil smells of butter!" But are you, and the Italian, and the Chinese really unlike?

In research for books of recreation based on life in other lands I found a curious similarity in games, stories, even in jokes. Perhaps the Africans who listened to our Homer Rodeheaver's stories smiled and thought, "Ha! one of grandfather's favorite jokes!" Would it be interesting and helpful for your society to start an adventure in understanding, a discovery of the customs, the folk-lore, the music, the art, of other peoples?

But—be careful! You *can* get very sentimental over the ability of the Negro in Africa and still despise the "nigger" around the corner. How can you get acquainted with the people of other races and nationalities in your own community? What makes you willing to support missions to foreigners far away, and unwilling to be friends with the foreigner near-by? Does fear of him help to raise the barrier—fear that he might get your job or that his presence will lower the value of your real estate? Is your ill feeling caused by a flaw in his character, or did it grow out of the prejudices of your family, or something you read, or the influence of a movie with a foreign villain?

Of what are the barriers built? And why, to be practical, should they be broken down? To help people whom we pity, or in simple justice?

"Jesus was all right," said my little Jewish tailor. "Jesus was all right, but Christianity!—Bah! In old Russia I saw my people killed with knives the priests had blessed. Here, where I thought it would be different, my little girl cries, 'Papa, they won't play with me. They say, "You Jew! you killed the Christ!" Papa, I no kill the Christ! Who was the Christ?'"

Who *was* the Christ? An ardent church woman objects when her son goes into a Jewish drug-store. "The druggist is a fine fellow," the son says. "All Jews are tricky and sly," she insists. "Yet," says her son quietly, "there are eight hundred churches in this city alone for the worship of one who was a Jew."

Who *is* the Christ? An Aryan German?—a "true-blue American white Christian"? Ours, exclusively? Or shall we, by *conduct as well as conversation*, share Him with others? What do we have to share?

He was a Filipino—his face tanned like his shoes. He was our college classmate, but he tired of our laughter at his oddness and left the school. But before he left he turned on us and cried, "You! What makes you think you are superior? What do *you* have? Tall buildings? Fast cars? Things! What spiritual values do you have?"

I wish we hadn't laughed. I tremble at the resentment he took back to his island home. I regret our loss of values to which he might have opened our eyes.

We break down the barriers to help others, but what of our own need that they be destroyed? Can we be safe in a world of barriers? Is peace possible? Can we make it possible by passing from prejudice to understanding, from suspicion to comradeship? What can comradeship with people of other races and nationalities add to our lives?

Remember that the barriers that shut out others wall us in. Lives grow dull within walls. Souls shrivel.

In our country today there are over two hundred organizations spreading propaganda against "Catholics, kikes, niggers and all kinds of foreigners." Some of these organizations dare to call themselves Christian. What will the spread of their spirit do to our nation? What can *we* do to stop it?

Color lines are as dangerous as live wires. Only Christian action can erase them. Let's not just talk about it. What shall we do—right now?

Dr. Albert J. Anthony, a college-town pastor at Alma, Michigan, and one of the trustees of the International Society of Christian Endeavor, stimulated our thinking on the problems of our social order. He spoke of the rising crisis of class struggle, of the sit-down strikes, of the question of property rights versus labor rights, of employment insurance and old-age security. He reminded us of the problems arising out of such domestic crises as divorce and of the lowered standards of amusement and current literature.

Said Dr. Anthony, "We must see not only with the eyes of Christ, but with the spirit of Christ try to work our remedy. Not for personal gain but out of love. We say, in effect, 'Be sober! Not because I am going to profit if you keep sober but because you will be better off.'"

Well! We went into the educational conferences ready to explode with questions after those three introductory statements. I was in the group led by Miss Ruth Seabury, and we surely had plenty of discussion. We reached some very definite conclusions, too, which will be recorded in our report.

My second period conference (the second period is devoted to the practical methods of doing Christian Endeavor work and there were seventeen subjects to choose from!) was on "Christian Endeavor in the Total Program of the Church." It was led by Rev. Myron T. Hopper, Director of Young People's Work for the Disciples of Christ.

It was a two-day conference and that was a good thing, for there were many things left over from Saturday's conference which we took up this morning. When you begin to think of Christian Endeavor's responsibility to the local church, and the ways in which the society can co-operate with other organizations to make possible a well-balanced program for all the young people, you open up some very interesting possibilities.

The general Convention session in the Auditorium (My! I'm

glad it is air-conditioned!) was presided over by Mr. Harry G. Kuch, president of the Pennsylvania State Union. Mr. Rodeheaver sang a solo, "The Christ of the Cross," and the speaker was Dr. Homer P. Rainey, Director of the American Youth Commission of the American Council on Education.

This Commission is making a five-year study of the needs of young people and developing plans to meet those needs. He said that from the study several outstanding facts are emerging. I put down several things he said:

The world is youth-conscious. Totalitarian states like Russia, in which there are one hundred million young people under twenty-four years old, think of youth as chattels. England has just appointed a commission to study youth's needs.

The outstanding problem is that of finding employment for young people. In this country there are six millions from sixteen to twenty-five who are out of school and unemployed. Too, the trend of employment is changing. Ninety per cent of the jobs available require 'ittle or no skill—they are the routine operative type of jobs. Since there will be more 'eisure in the future young people will have to seek in other sources than employment for the major satisfactions of life.

It makes no difference what kind of program is developed for youth if ultimately they have to go to war.

The confusion of modern life—confusion in politics, in economics, and in science—makes life difficult for youth. They are bewildered by apparently changing moral standards and ideals.

Young people are at their best:
1. When they are seeing visions;
2. When they have faith to translate their visions into reality;
3. When they live for others;
4. When they are fired with a high moral passion;
5. When they are filled with enthusiasm for true objects of devotion;
6. When they are seriously and resolutely following the way of Christ.

Today's radio talk by Dr. Poling was a sequel to his talk on Saturday when he described the dangerous, warlike marching of youth in many countries. He said:

Today the alternative to the mobilization of youth for warlike purposes is the appeal of Jesus, who alone has a program. Following the program of Jesus young people would march, not against each other but with each other for social good, for better living conditions, for a wider spread of the blessings of life.

The program of Jesus is desperately hard. Jesus is a harder leader to follow than Hitler or Mussolini or Stalin. *He* says, "If any man would come after me, let him take up his cross and follow me." *He* says, "*Love* your enemies." The program of Jesus is incredibly hard, but Jesus is irresistibly attractive.

In a museum in Topeka, Kansas, is a little card. On one side of it is a cross and the Lord's Prayer; on the reverse is the Christian Endeavor pledge. There are brown spots on the card. This is its history:

During the Boxer Rebellion the Boxers came to the mission at Tientsin and found that everyone had left except a lad twelve years old. The soldiers gave him his choice—to give up the card and his belief in Christ, and so save his life, or to keep it and lose his head. The Marines a little later found his headless body, but the card was clasped in his hand.

Photo by Lee F. Redman, Detroit
MISS SARAH E. McCULLAGH
Detroit, Michigan
Region No. 4

MRS. H. SPENCER CLARK
Scarborough, Ontario
Region No. 8

MRS. FRANCES KREEGER
Atlanta, Georgia
Region No. 3

Regional Vice Presidents

(Those chosen in three districts were unable to accept, and their successors are yet to be chosen)

RALPH W. ARNOLD
Brockton, Massachusetts
Region No. 1

REUEL B. WOLFORD
Wilkinsburg, Pennsylvania
Region No. 2

Photo by Bachrach
BANCROFT REIFSNYDER
San Angel, Mexico
Region No. 9

"I choose Christ!" is more than a motto!

Is it possible to see Jesus clearly?

Channing Pollock, the playwright, told Dr. Charles Sheldon and me at a luncheon one day how the writer, Basil King, had called him a fool because he had never read the life of Christ in the Gospels Said Pollock. "I went home and read it twice, then fell on my knees and prayed. When I arose I was passionately in love with Jesus Christ, and every line that I have written since has been propaganda for some good cause."

There is an alternative! It is the Christian program for the new world!

This afternoon was free unless you belonged to one of the states —Wisconsin, Michigan, or Indiana—holding its annual convention. Being from New York we had no scheduled meeting, so we spent some time in the Exhibition Hall, then looked over the books. (I bought "So This Is Missions!" by Stock, and the basic pamphlets in the "Christian Youth Building a New World" materials.)

Then I took a nap. It seemed a waste of time, but I've been on the go every second since last Wednesday, with only very few hours to sleep at night. I felt like new after the nap, so I dressed and went over to Mr. Rodeheaver's conference on "Religious Music and Song Direction." Very interesting and helpful, and "Rody" is a scream! He makes you laugh, but you learn while you are laughing!

No special dinner tonight, so we ate in the Hotel Pantlind cafeteria. (Delicious cake for dessert!)

Then the evening session, another memorable experience—stirring music, a brief but vital worship service, and then a period which was exciting and challenging and jolly all at once, and which made us all seem like one huge Christian Endeavor family.

We heard the report of the Trustees' Meeting and the result of the election of officers for the International Society of Christian Endeavor. (The whole report will be given in the Convention Report.) Most important is the re-election of Dr. Poling as President and the election of Arthur J. Stanley of Oregon as Associate President. He is only twenty-six! He is not here because he was sent to represent Christian Endeavor at the World Conference of Churches (Church, Community and State) in Oxford, England. Mrs. Stanley was presented to the audience in his place. She has been Mrs. Stanley just one month! (This Convention is full of Christian Endeavor romances!)

The nine Regional Vice-presidents just elected by the Board of Trustees were not all present tonight. Those who were received plenty of applause. So did the superintendents of departments of Christian Endeavor work.

Then Dr. Poling announced the names of those who had registered already for the next Convention. I could hardly believe it, but there were more than a dozen who registered at once, each paying two dollars. If it hadn't been so near to the end of this convention, with my pocketbook so flat, I'd have done it myself. I intend to go, though.

We were so full of enthusiasm by this time that when the appeal for financial subscriptions to carry on Christian Endeavor work was made, there was a splendid response. Nearly twelve thousand dollars was pledged for the coming year. All who pledged at least twelve dollars are to be called "Comrades for the Crisis."

You wouldn't think any speaker would want to try to bring a serious message to a crowd that was somewhat excited and a little tired. Dr. Peale did—and it was wonderful. He made us laugh even harder than we had laughed, and then he swung our emotions from laughter to intense concern about the possibilities of using spiritual power. His address is to be in the Official Report so I didn't take it down. I just listened.

How thankful I am for shorthand to make it possible for me to record these days! What a day this has been!

Thank you, God, for all this Convention means to me!

DR. POLING INTRODUCES AND GIVES HIS CONGRATULATIONS TO MISS DONNA CHAPPELL OF MEMPHIS, MO., AND MR. RONALD KEELER, OF BLOOMSBURG, PA. THESE TWO YOUNG PEOPLE WERE CHOSEN BY *The Lookout* AS WINNERS IN AN EFFORT TO DISCOVER IN THE ENTIRE BROTHERHOOD OF THE DISCIPLES OF CHRIST THOSE WHO WERE OUTSTANDINGLY USEFUL TO THEIR LOCAL CHURCHES IN 1936. THE RECORDS OF ATTAINMENT OF MISS CHAPPELL AND MR. KEELER ARE AMAZINGLY FINE.

V

We Face the Future

Tuesday

WHEN Tuesday came, no one thought of it as the *last* day. True, it was the final day of the Convention, but it was the Day That Faced Forward! Convention was ending in Grand Rapids, but all that Convention had stimulated us to be and to do was just about to begin in thousands of different places!

On this Day That Faced Forward delegates rose early in order to miss no precious moment. The morning Quiet Hour was crowded. It began as it had begun every morning, with the Twenty-third Psalm and the Lord's Prayer. "Jesus Calls Us," sang the Convention. Dr. Frederick W. Norwood then spoke of how Jesus had called Paul.

Could we bear what Paul had borne? More than one delegate asked himself this question. Could we endure seeing all our safe, respectable, honored life swept away; having our old friends shrink from us and the people whose company we had joined suspect our motives? Could we, in our time, make of our discipleship of Jesus a thrilling adventure?

Three young people spoke in the introductory conference session. The theme for the day was "Christ Meeting the World's Needs," the last theme to be considered in the Convention's study of "Christian Youth Building a New World." Preceding these three speakers Dr. Albert J. Anthony spoke briefly. Said Dr. Anthony:

"We must live dangerously, for our world is a small and dangerous world. It takes longer to draw a line around a golf ball than it does to flash a message around the world. The world of nations is dangerously *friendly;* the danger of war grows out of secret intrigues and treaties and strategy. The nations of this world are dangerously *self-sufficient.* The totalitarian states are conserving their resources for future emergencies. Democracy declines. We must recommit ourselves to the great unfinished tasks. We must have Christian statesmen, since only Christ can meet the world's needs. Missions must continue, with missionaries committed to social action. We must play our part in making a Christian world possible."

Mr. Ernest R. Bryan, Superintendent of the World Peace Fellowship of Christian Endeavor, said:

I have been asked to state what my own personal views on peace are. The greatest inspiration of my life was the Christian Endeavor Convention in Berlin, in 1930, when youth met on the platform. "We will be friends." Delegates there

47

were willing to discuss the causes of the World War, facing facts instead of dodging facts

My views are my own, not those of any organization. I believe: first, that peace is possible; that it is inevitable if youth will demand it; second, that peace is desirable; that war settles nothing. I believe that we should solve international problems with brains, not with bullets! Third, that peace is essential, for the world cannot stand another major war. I believe in collective security, in such institutions as the World Court.

I would not participate in any war. I should like to fight war itself instead of fighting people.

Lieut. Victor Mansfield, a recent graduate of the U. S. Military Academy, West Point, spoke on world friendship. Said Lieut. Mansfield:

One year ago the U.S. Army transport "Chateau Thierry" steamed sluggishly through the middle Atlantic, and two "Kaydets" hung over the rail facing a burning sunset—and with an occasional dream of a girl back home! How much that sea resembled life in breadth and depth! It fascinated our imagination.

Suddenly we two amateur philosophers felt the push of a squall on our backs. A real storm was trailing our wake! What a thrill! Some sort of excitement at last! Plunging and plowing we tossed past a couple of liners to port. Not a chance of hitting. We had the best captain in the service for our ship. We had *a steady hand at the wheel*—an able man on the bridge! These men knew the sea. They were powerful, confident, capable—ready for any emergency! To the last man we felt secure that night!

When world-wide troubles come, don't we need just this? Our forefathers were God-fearing men. They brought the greatest democracy of history through every crisis by honest toil. Washington, Lincoln, Theodore Roosevelt and many others—how we honor what they did! Each a Christian—asking God's guidance and receiving it for our country! *They* were *steady hands at the wheel!* Do we not need this for all governments?

When economic depressions and struggles for racial unity bring war in Europe, do we feel secure? When a dynamic power like Germany, Italy, or Japan tries for national necessities by force, don't we feel we must revive the weakening machinery for world friendship—the League World Court, and any practical solution?

Yet we know in our hearts the solution—the only way—the way that cannot fail! With men of God in all areas of international life, would not world friendship of nations be assured? Don't we need men of courage, men who dare—Christians—in business, politics, and economic fields, as leaders—Christians who put loyalty in their duty—always receiving power and guidance from a Christ for the Crisis—and with His love in their hearts? With all governments under a steady hand at the wheel, we know world friendship would be inevitable!

Miss Rose Y. Zenn of Ambridge, Pennsylvania, gave the last talk in this period. Miss Zenn said:

I am marching with Christ as the great Commander-in-chief of the army against war.

Peace!—what connotations come to me as I think of it! First, the knowledge of the fact that I am a pacifist. How do I know that I am? I feel it in my heart. Then, while taking a class at the University of Pittsburgh during the last fall semester, the professor gave us a test which determined to a degree whether or not one was a pacifist or a belligerent. I was anxious to learn the results of my responses. and was greatly pleased, for I registered a pacifist almost to the extreme. Nor would I have become too alarmed had I registered a fanatic for peace!

Another connotation is the story of "The Christ of the Andes." The countries of Chile and Argentina were preparing to wage a great war against each other. A certain bishop, mindful of the preparations being made, preached from his pulpit on an Easter Sunday a sermon on brotherly love and the ideals of peace set forth by the Prince of Peace. So eloquently and with such zeal did he preach that his words greatly moved his hearers and spread like wildfire to both sides. Preparations for war ceased, by arbitration. All the guns, bullets, cannons, and other war implements of both sides were gathered together and placed in a great receptacle and melted. Out of this was made the mammoth statute of Christ and placed high in the Andes on the boundary line between the two countries. There it can be seen today and there it stands as a constant reminder that the people of these two countries may have slaughtered each other at one time, but that the Prince of Peace now reigns supreme in their relations.

Oh, that all nations today would collect all the guns, the bullets, the cannons, and all the other implements—yes, the battleships and airplanes—and pour over these the deadly chemicals that have been invented and concocted to exterminate life, and entire cities at a time, and erect a monument to one great love and Brotherhood of Man and for peace eternal!

We as youth need peace education. There is an appalling inertia and ignorance with respect to all matters that pertain to peace and a chronic indisposition to become informed. Also, we have deeply ingrained "mind sets" to overcome in order to build the mind to peace. You heard Dr. Louis Evans say that we have peace in our minds but not in our hearts, and that is where we must get it to truly go forward.

But education is not enough. It is too slow. Perhaps eventually education may build a peaceful world, but the problem now is to hold war at bay, first to save this generation—you and me—from being engulfed in war. Second, to give education a chance to get its work done. The need of the very moment is action, peace action, that is intelligent, realistic, and drastic. I am ready to act. Are you?

The time of the educational conferences seemed much too short. Delegates were consoled only by the thought of continuing to learn through the books recommended for study and through discussion groups formed in their own communities.

Dr. P. Frank Price, President of the Christian Endeavor Union of China, was the speaker at the General Convention session in the morning. Before his talk Mr. Rodeheaver led the Convention in singing "Fairest Lord Jesus" and "Faith of Our Fathers," and himself sang as a solo, "When My Dreams Come True."

For forty-seven years Dr. Price has been a missionary to China. His message therefore came to the Convention with the authority of long experience. He said:

The Chinese are one-fourth of the total population of the world. Today they are our near neighbors, for the journey to China which seventy years ago took six months, can now be made in ten days. The Chinese are a great people. Given a chance, a Chinese boy or girl will rise to the top in any group. They are a people of great endurance. This is expressed by the little boy who was shivering and who replied to the question, "Are you cold?" "Yes, I am cold, but it is only three months until spring." China needs endurance, as she is beset by banditry, civil war, misrule, poverty, and the evils of superstition, and now is menaced by a cruel and unjust war.

China is the land of the open door. This was not always so. For centuries the door was barred and bolted. Today there are Christians in every stratum of society. The struggle for religious liberty was a long, hard struggle, but liberty of conscience is embodied in law today. John Hay, Secretary of State, announced the policy of the open door for commerce.

There is great opportunity for Christian Endeavor in China. It is now found in thirty denominations in China and in twenty-seven states or provinces. Christian Endeavor stretches to the far west boundary. Its work is done without fear of bandits or heat or cold. Three men in the Shanghai office are working sacrificially to promote it. The Secretary of Christian Endeavor, Mr. A. T. Y. Chow, was educated in Canada and is a capable, efficient worker. He now works as a volunteer. I hope to take back the word that he can be supported for full time service.

God's word for Christian Endeavor in China is the word He spoke to the Israelites, "Go Forward!"

What a thrill it was, after Dr. Price's address, to have Dr. Poling read a greeting from the Chinese Christian Endeavor Union and then announce that the money was available to support Mr. Chow as General Secretary for Christian Endeavor in China! On the vote of the Convention a cablegram was sent promptly to Mr. Chow, telling him the good news.

Mr. Carroll M. Wright then presented the awards won in the Grand Rapids registration campaign, which began in May, 1936.

Utah won the honor of leading the convention parade, and Honor Banner No. 1 with 153 per cent of her quota; Georgia was second in the parade and was awarded Honor Banner No. 2, with 152 per cent. Florida was awarded third place and Honor Banner No. 3 with 104 per cent. Then the following States, in order, were awarded the next places in the parade and numbered banners of a smaller size than the first three—Washington, Pennsylvania, Kansas, Maryland, the Golden Rule Union (Washington, D. C., Negro), and Tennessee.

The Philadelphia County Union took the lead among the local unions of the country and was awarded Local Union Honor Banner No. 1 for having secured a total of 100 registrations. The South Central District Union of Kansas was awarded Local Union Honor Banner No. 2.

Honor was paid to a number of individuals who had secured large numbers of registrations. The leaders among these individual workers were:

	Registrations
Richard R. Fry, Glenolden, Pa.	118
Miss Myrtle Clausen, Peoria, Ill.	63
Miss Gladys Gray, Newton, Kans.	61

Miss Patricia Piper, Milwaukee, Wis. . . 60
Miss Catherine Ritchie, Washington, D. C. 53
James A. Brown, Golden Rule Union, Washington, D. C. 52
Mrs. Mary F. Brown, Golden Rule Union, Washington,
 D. C. 51
Rolla M. Varndell, Uniontown, Pa. . . 51

Mr. Martin Harvey brought to the Convention the greetings of the Christian Youth Council of North America.

Young People's Radio Conference

Mr. W. Roy Breg presided at the Radio Conference and Dr. Poling spoke on "The Equation of Victory." Said Dr. Poling:

I shall repeat an equation I talked about many years ago. It is this: Inspiration + Information × Perspiration = Consummation or Victory.

Inspiration must be undergirded by information.

I have always believed in the young people of this country. I believe in them more than ever, in spite of what I sometimes see and hear. The few disreputable youth make the most noise. We may mistake what a few say, for fact.

To illustrate this:—sometime ago the conversation in a Pullman dressing room concerned Billy Sunday. "Billy Sunday leads a double life," one man announced. The others would have accepted that statement as a fact, had there not been a direct contradiction from one who *knew*. William Allen White, famous editor of *The Emporia Gazette*, was able to give the true facts.

Information has been poured into this Convention on race, peace, social security, fundamental Americanism. Inspired as never before, we may apply this information in our own churches, societies, and unions.

Talking about the inspiration which lasts, in this Convention we have had an inspired leadership plus an inspired rank and file. We have had an illustration of "multiplied by perspiration"—or hard work—in the Utah delegation which comes, as a large percentage of Utah's membership, to this gathering. We have seen the great delegation from Pennsylvania, a result of hard work. We have seen the results of the work of the Grand Rapids Convention Committee. We thank the people of Grand Rapids for their hospitality, including the trip to Holland, and for the use of this magnificent, cool auditorium. We thank the city officials and the newspapers of Grand Rapids for their appreciative presentation of the Convention.

Consummation, triumph. We saw an illustration of that last night. If we believe, the mountain of the world's problems shall come tumbling down. In the play, "The Fool," a sick child asks, "Can I be well if I believe?" and the answer comes, "Yes, *if you believe hard enough!*" If we believe hard enough there are things we can do in race, peace, and all the other areas of effort in building a new world.

> I do not ask, O Lord, a life all free from pain;
> I do not seek to be in this great world of need
> Without my load of care; for this I know,
> The present cross is my eternal gain
> And he who struggles, battles on,
> At last shall enter in and be a victor there.
> So, Lord, just keep me fit within
> And give me strength to fight;
> And I shall follow through the din
> From darkness up to light.

The Closing Session

Tuesday afternoon was so pleasantly occupied by the trip to Holland and the picnic supper that Tuesday night came all too soon.

Dr. Poling himself presided at this final meeting of the Convention. Never were hymns sung with more heartfelt meaning than in the opening song period. Never could a song leader draw forth more beautifully blended melody. Never did a Convention choir contribute music which more clearly expressed the spiritual emotion of the delegates.

The worship service, "The Consecration of Paul" (in perfect harmony with Dr. Norwood's message at the morning Quiet Hour) was led by Rev. Edward P. Downey, pastor of Westminster Presbyterian Church, Grand Rapids. Then a trio, the Vandermeulen sisters, Bernice, and Ruth and Esther (twins) sang "Near to the Heart of God."

A cablegram of greeting was voted to be sent to the two Christian Endeavor representatives at the World Conference on Life and Work of the Churches, at Oxford, England, Clark V. Poling and Arthur J. Stanley. It was announced that cablegrams had been sent to Mr. Chow of China and to Mr. Abbey of India, telling of the victorious financial program.

Mr. Carroll M. Wright read the following telegram from Dr. William Shaw, former General Secretary of the International Society of Christian Endeavor:

The church and world were never more in need of the kind of young people Christian Endeavor trains than today. Success to all your efforts. Heartiest thanks for your cordial greeting.

WILLIAM SHAW.

Then Dr. Poling introduced the Chairman of the Convention Committee, Mr. George Veldman, who presented his father and mother and each member of the Convention Committee. Enthusiastic applause greeted these people who had done so much to make the Convention a success.

Mr. Wright awarded the prizes for the winning delegations in the Convention parade. (See Chapter X.)

Dr. Poling introduced to the audience Mrs. Catherine Miller Balm, Recorder of the Convention, and Mr. Gene Stone, in charge of Convention publicity. Miss Mildreth Haggard, Junior Superintendent, was unable to be present, but was paid a grateful tribute by President Poling. Mrs. Poling needed no introduction, but the delegates were glad to have her presented at this time so that they might express their affection in applause.

The Call to Australia

Although not many delegates from this Continent could hope to attend the next World's Convention because of the expense of travel, the call to that Convention was heard eagerly. Dr. Poling read:

Tenth Convention

WORLD'S CHRISTIAN ENDEAVOR UNION

═══ Official Call ═══

To Christian Endeavorers in Every Land

Greetings!

IN THE NAME OF THE CHRISTIAN ENDEAVORERS OF AUSTRALIA AND NEW ZEALAND, we, the officers of the World's Christian Endeavor Union and co-operating National Christian Endeavor Unions, invite the Christian Endeavorers from all lands to attend the Tenth World's Christian Endeavor Convention, to be held in Melbourne, Australia, August 2 to 8, 1938.

We would convene in the spirit of Him who said, "By this shall all men know that ye are my disciples, if ye have love one to another." We would make vital in the life of Christian Endeavor in all the world, and in its world organization, the leadership of Christ in personal living, in evangelism, in Christian education, in Christian citizenship and in Christian brotherhood.

The world sorely needs the message of this convention and its application to all of man's necessities. We are challenged to Christianize the social order and to build the new and Christian world.

The convention theme will be "The Challenge of Christ to Youth—Follow Me!"

The convention program will include all phases of Christian Endeavor testimony, organization, and service.

The Australasian officers and Endeavorers cordially invite us in the name of our common Lord, and open to us their hearts and homes. Let the nations respond!

Further particulars may be had from the secretary, Dr. Stanley B. Vandersall, 41 Mount Vernon Street, Boston, Massachusetts, U. S. A.

Finally, we call upon our four million Endeavorers and millions more of their friends of all lands, all tongues, all races, and all evangelical churches to unite with us in prayer for the success of this world gathering.

Daniel A. Poling
President

Geo. H. Nelson
Vice-president

James Kelly
Vice-president

Harry S. Holmes
Honorary Secretary

Stanley B. Vandersall
Secretary-Treasurer

WORLD'S CHRISTIAN ENDEAVOR BUILDING
Boston, Massachusetts, U. S. A.

"For Christ and the Church"

Not many could go to Melbourne, but everybody wanted to go, especially after Mr. Harry N. Holmes, born in Australia, spoke of his native land and of what the World's Convention would mean to Australia.

Mr. Paul C. Brown, new General Representative for the International Society, spoke of the importance to Endeavorers of *The Christian Endeavor World*, and forcefully and successfully presented the matter of subscriptions.

Mr. Rodeheaver played "The Holy City" on his trombone while the generous offering of the evening was being received. Then the Convention rose to sing, "We Choose Christ."

Dr. Frederick Norwood, of London, England, put all the power of his persuasive eloquence into his address. It moved the tense audience to sincere heart-searching and to definite commitment to the "larger liberty and deeper life" made possible by the power of Christ. (Dr. Norwood's address appears in Chapter VI.)

It was not strange that after such an address many young people, who had not made decisions to accept Jesus or for full-time Christian service on Sunday night, were glad to accept Dr. Poling's call to do so at this time. They went eagerly to the platform and the prayers of their fellow delegates went with them.

Hands linked, the delegates stood to sing "God Be With You, Till We Meet Again." Hands linked in fellowship, hearts linked in love of Christ, their Leader, minds linked in the high purpose of going forth to face the future with courage, to do their part in building a Christian world, in proving the power of *Christ for the Crisis*.

THE USHERS PASS THE REVIEWING STAND

VI

We Hear Inspiring Addresses

To MANY delegates the high points of a convention are the addresses made by men and women of wide Christian experience and inspiring eloquence. "Grand Rapids, 1937" gave us many memorable addresses.

No record of words spoken can convey the magnetic charm of a speaker's personality—the quiet earnestness of Admiral Byrd, the twinkle in the eyes of Dr. Frederick Norwood, the passionate sincerity of Dr. Louis Evans, the ability of Dr. Norman Peale to swing an audience from the ridiculous to the sublime. One must have the impact of personality to know exactly what a speech can mean. To those who were in Grand Rapids memory will make the words of the speeches given here ring with reality. To those who can only read the words—why, the words are well worth reading! Some of them may speak directly to your heart. And perhaps at the next convention you, too, may meet these speakers.

Addresses Made at Evening Sessions

THURSDAY EVENING

"Peace," an address by Rear Admiral Richard Evelyn Byrd, U. S. N. (Retired), is quoted in Chapter II.

Richard Evelyn Byrd was born in Virginia. He has served with distinction as a naval officer. His transatlantic flight and his North Pole and Antarctic explorations have been exploits of high courage, yielding invaluable scientific information. His books describing his experiences are fascinating tales of heroic adventure.

FRIDAY EVENING

"Christ for the Crisis," by Rev. Daniel A. Poling, D.D., LL.D., is quoted here in full.

Daniel A. Poling was born in Oregon and began preaching at the age of eighteen. He is a graduate of Dallas College and Ohio State University. His first pastorate was in Canton, Ohio. He was a chaplain and Y.M.C.A. worker in the World War. Dr. Poling has been pastor of Marble Collegiate Church, New York City, and is now pastor of the Baptist Temple, Philadelphia. He is editor of *Christian Herald* and President of the International Society of Christian Endeavor. As President of the World's Christian Endeavor Union, he has traveled around the world. Dr. Poling is a celebrated radio speaker and has written many interesting books.

55

Christ for the Crisis

CHRISTIAN ENDEAVOR came to the church providentially for a crisis time in the life of youth. This fact, and no other, explains the rapid rise and world-wide development of the movement. Francis E. Clark was the chosen leader, God's man to release, to organize, and to guide this ministry over the earth. Christian Endeavor has continued to increase its activities and grow in membership because it has not ceased to serve a vital need. With a minimum of organizational equipment, often with considerably less than the required minimum of financial support, it has added numbers, expanded in service, and grown in spiritual power.

Certainly it has not been immune to the recessions that all organizations at times experience. Whole countries have suffered reverses and some utter eclipse Entire churches have withdrawn from the fellowship At the moment, the movement in Germany, in Spain, and in certain of the Baltic and Balkan countries is passing through extreme ordeals.

Reverses and Triumphs

On the other hand, reverses in these lands are matched by achievements in others. As I speak to you, Christian Endeavor in Japan, with only slight assistance from the United States, is experiencing a renaissance. By a special gift, the Church of Christ in China is collaborating with the International Society of Christian Endeavor in a distinctive educational experiment. The Korean church is using Christian Endeavor as perhaps no other single communion or country ever before has. India, under the guidance of the Abbeys, is in the midst of unifying the activities of the Epworth League and Christian Endeavor. Australia reports a total membership of more than one hundred thousand and has become numerically, from the standpoint of national population, the most powerful single national unit within our fellowship. The United Kingdom continues her sound and constructive program—a program that comprehends all departments of our work. There has been encouraging progress in Hungary. Among the countries that offer us particularly inviting opportunities are Rumania, Yugoslavia, Italy and France.

World's Convention

Following Grand Rapids, our next great convention landmark is Melbourne, Australia, August 2-8, 1938—next summer. The Australian National Committee is composed of a remarkable group of men and women, representative of both church life and public affairs. Plans already made have more generously regarded the needs of the World's Christian Endeavor Union than those of any other similar gathering. It is our earnest hope that a representative delegation will go out to Australia from the United States and that there may be a large general movement from all other countries.

This will be the first international gathering of our society ever held in Australasia. Associated with it is the opportunity for some to attend the missionary conference in Hangchow, China, which promises to be the most prophetic Christian gathering ever convened in the Orient.

World Tour

Your President's recent world tour, which carried him into forty-six countries or islands, emphasized the strategic position of the Far East in the Kingdom task of the generation and century immediately before us. Christian Endeavor is in a strategic position to make contributions to a new occasion for Christ and for the church, to develop and enrich youth life, to prepare young men and young women for the Kingdom enterprise in the Far East.

I was accompanied on this world visitation by Mrs. Poling and our fellow Trustee, Miss Helen L. Lyon. Mrs. Poling and Miss Lyon made their own contributions to the visitation. Their presence was everywhere a blessing to the missionary enterprise in general, as it was to Christian Endeavor in particular.

May I add here that at the suggestion of Mother Clark herself a Mother's Christian Endeavor Society has been organized in my own church with Mrs. Poling as leader. The society has been given Mother Clark's own name, though not at her suggestion. It is a conversational group made up first of mothers of the young men in one of our Sunday School classes which is contributing annually $600 toward Christian Endeavor in Japan. To these have been added others, until the group numbers about thirty, meeting each Sunday evening to discuss Christian Endeavor principles, history and program. I think it is the first organization of its kind.

This world tour has not only given your President a more intelligent understanding of our movement's needs and increased his faith in the genius of its organizational plan; it has confirmed him in the conclusion that the fundamental principles of Christian Endeavor are as timely now as they were fifty years ago; that the departments of our work—Junior, Intermediate, Young People's, Adult, with graded activities, the Quiet Hour, the Tenth Legion, Life-work Recruits, the alumni, and the whole educational scheme, which has kept pace with the latest developments in the curriculum of the church, comprehend the requirements of the field in which we operate, and that they are required now if the church herself is to be well served with youth training and leadership.

I believed in Christian Endeavor when I began this visitation; my belief had taken on proportions of new understanding when the journey was completed with our arrival in San Francisco.

Reorganization

Organizational work on the North American continent has experienced the handicaps of contingent financial stringency but in spite of poverty, or perhaps blessed by it, state after state has renewed and even enlarged the service program. There are tonight more field secretaries employed than there were two years ago.

Particularly significant during the past year has been the work of the Reorganization Committee, which, receiving recommendations from the president, has gone forward along these and along other original lines to prepare a report which has won the favorable action of your Executive Committee. This report is now before the Trustees. It will, I believe, command the enthusiastic support of this convention and of our movement throughout the continent. The recommendations of the report, when they become operative, will bring the young people themselves into the direction of our movement, into the responsibilities of its program and into the opportunities of its leadership as never before in the history of Christian Endeavor. With my executive associates, I rejoice in the prophetic steps that are now to be taken.

Immediately before us is the problem of debt, but this problem may be mentioned now with words of hope. The Craigie Manor properties have been sold. Provision has been made for new income through the tapping of new sources and by the establishing of a new financial department.

The Christian Endeavor World

The Christian Endeavor World, restored to the monthly basis and with particularly intimate State relationships, enters, we believe, upon a new era of service to our movement. As a service organ, it should be in this time what the Golden Rule and its successor became in the past generation of our growth

United Action

The program released from this Convention to the States, through the youth departments of all co-operating youth agencies and through the individual societies of the churches within our fellowship, will bear not only the imprimatur of our International Headquarters—it will be the co-operative achievement of both denominational and interdenominational representatives.

Certainly we have not as yet achieved perfection of procedure; we are conscious of limitations and of mistakes. But we are determined to make definite progress toward a unity of spirit in program and action that shall serve all our interests an advance always the interests of the task itself. We shall continue our co-operation with those projects and campaigns that move across the field we occupy, with all other youth agencies and with all other groups having common cause with us and serving the total Christian task.

The United Christian Youth Movement offers us generally a point of contact and a clearing-house. All plans must, of course, in their application be adapted to the needs of State and local unions. In particular instances, the question of leadership and emphasis has presented a problem. Always Christian Endeavor should and, we believe, will remain true to her evangelical ideals and her organizational principles. We shall not sacrifice these for the mere appearance of unity. Christian Endeavor is not a young people's church; Christian Endeavor is an agency of the church and operating within the church. "For Christ and the Church" is more than a motto—it is a service creed.

Peace

We shall continue to promote the program for world peace launched in Philadelphia two years ago. It is my earnest hope that this program may be vitalized and given aggressive leadership as a result of financial plans just now being inaugurated. With a comparatively small expenditure we can, I believe, capitalize the greatest peace opportunity offered any organization.

Our principle of unity as against uniformity is now generally recognized by peace organizations and advocates. The Emergency Peace Campaign has been and is a practical demonstration of this principle. Our purpose to have a part in uniting all organizations and all peace-makers of all shades and degrees in support of those measures that represent the full length of our common agreements is strengthened by recent developments. Surely no organization in the world has a greater stake in peace than has Christian Endeavor.

I call to your attention tonight our Philadelphia platform. I challenge you to reaffirm it here and to give it the support that will carry it over the world. No presentation made on our world visitation received a more eager response, a more enthusiastic endorsement, than this.

Temperance

Temperance education and legislation command our attention. The growing menace of liquor is a challenge to Christian citizens in every state in the union, in every city and on every countryside. Repeal has been and increasingly is a tragic, a monstrous failure. Every promise made by its proponents has been broken, every hope of its friends has died. The rising tide of liquor consumption, law violation, drinking among men, women and children, slaughter on the highways, juvenile delinquency and a new approach to political corruption through new ventures in liquor control, are sweeping toward a social disaster.

So apparent is the acceleration of this movement that warning voices are raised in the trade itself. Liquor manufacturers are fairly shouting in their advertisements, that liquor is not a necessity and that it must not require money that should be spent for necessities. In certain State Legislatures, liquor dealers' associations have urged the enactment of regulatory measures to mitigate the evils that grow more apparent day by day.

While there is a wide variance of opinion as to the total responsibility of drinking for serious and fatal highway accidents, there is general agreement that here liquor has a constantly increasing part. In 1936 nearly one million people were injured and more than thirty-six thousand were killed on the streets and roads of America. If the rate of increase for the first quarter of 1937 is continued, the total fatalities of 1937 will reach fifty thousand.

The open sale of alcoholic beverages has reached scandalous proportions. President Franklin D. Roosevelt in his first inaugural address said: "The saloon must not return. By no possibility, at any time or under any conditions, at any place, or under any circumstances, shall that institution the saloon or its equivalent be allowed to return to American life."

The President spoke in good faith; his words expressed his purpose. But there are now more than four hundred seventy-three thousand places of liquor-sale in the United States, three hundred thousand more than in saloon days. In tens of thousands of these, minors of both sexes are served freely, while young women for the first time in modern American history are employed as barmaids. Again and again these places are inexcusably worse than the old saloon.

Once again Christian Endeavor with all her resources must engage in the struggle for a sober nation. A world largely mechanized cannot afford to mix alcohol and gasoline. A democracy confronted by the economic and social ordeals that all but overwhelm us dares not unsteady the hand and becloud the mind of her sovereign ruler with alcohol unrestrained and fed to private profit.

We call upon Christian Endeavor unions to emulate Michigan Christian Endeavorers in advocating the passage of anti-liquor advertising bills.

We call upon our young people everywhere to enlist in such activities as those of Allied Youth, and to unite with all other agencies of like mind and purpose to promote total abstinence by choice of the individual; prohibition in every unit, large and small, that may be captured by free votes of the people; and for the complete destruction of the liquor traffic for profit.

We Believe in America

In this and in similar activities, we shall advance the interests of fundamental Americanism—Americanism with its republican form of democratic government, as against totalitarianism of every sort and degree. Neither Communism nor Fascism has any place on this free soil. We believe in what we now possess and in the larger good we may achieve. Not by fear, but by faith, shall we go forward. Wrongs there are, and they must be righted; inequalities continue that must be removed. But all voices that are lifted to set one class against another or to exploit weakness for selfish political advantage should be answered by an aroused civic conscience, constant in its support of unselfish public servants and always standing guard at the polls on election day.

Indifference is the only foe that can finally defeat American democracy—the indifference of the private citizen. Against this indifference the citizenship activities of Christian Endeavor will be directed through the next two years. Here let us be reminded by Justice Brandeis, that "experience should teach us to be most on guard to protect liberty when purposes of government are beneficent. Men born to freedom are naturally alert to repel invasion of their liberty by evil-minded persons, but the greatest dangers to liberty lurk in insidious encroachment by men of zeal, well-meaning but without understanding."

The Courts

This American freedom depends upon the maintenance of its safeguards. Freedom must be watchful, freedom must be zealous. Another has said, and well said, history proves that the greatest safeguard of freedom is the independent court. Let America treasure and hold inviolate this independence.

Genius of Christian Endeavor

Two things remain to be said: First, a re-emphasis on the genius of Christian Endeavor, and finally, our re-statement of the place of Christian Endeavor and of the church herself in the present world crisis.

The supreme business of Christian Endeavor is leading young people to Jesus Christ, bringing them into the life of the church, training them there for the service of Christ and His cause through all human relationships. Let the Grand Rapids Convention re-affirm this faith and reorganize Christian Endeavor departments to carry forward its complete plan. Evangelism, the Quiet Hour, the Tenth Legion, the study of the whole missionary enterprise, and the entire program of Christian education should receive from us a fresh evaluation. Let us go out from this prophetic gathering to lead a hundred thousand of our youthful associates to Jesus Christ and to enroll as many in the Quiet Hour and the Tenth Legion.

Under the program prepared for us by the Reorganization Committee, we shall have departmental leadership that should give our movement hundreds of new Junior and Intermediate Christian Endeavor societies and that should revitalize every department of our program. For the first time, young men and young women—you, all of you, and all of your associates at home—are to be directly responsible for Christian Endeavor's forward march. Into your hands is to be given the opportunity of leadership, and with the opportunity comes the sacred obligation to achieve.

The Nations

"Christ for the Crisis" is our motto and our convention theme. Already we have intimated a crisis in the state, in the social order, in the community, but consider some of the particulars of the crisis among the nations. Again civilization peels her thin veneer. Today Spain, where hundreds of our comrades suffer, is the proving ground of the latest torture devices of so-called Christian nations. A generation ago one power declared a single treaty to be a scrap of paper. Today few powers have not violated, within the lifetime of the government that assumed them, the most solemn international engagements. Europe may be likened to a hospital with the psychopathic ward threatening to take over the operating room. With the checks and balances of democracy thrown off, revolution, counter-revolution, international banditry, and presently a general war, wait only on the mood and the word of a dictator.

My overseas visitation brought to me the disquieting conclusion that no country and no race has escaped the inoculation of fear and distrust. Today over the world statesmen play with bloody chess, war captains manoeuver, and always youth marches. We would not lift our voices in blame tonight, for all have sinned.

What of the Protestant Church?

But in the light of the facts that constitute the world crisis, what of the church? A denominational publication recently said editorially, "Opposing the church today are forces too powerful and too united for a weak and a divided church."

Well, if this is true, and if the world is as disturbed as I believe it to be. Protestant Christianity, far from being in position to conduct a successful offensive, may be presently unable to maintain her own position.

A little more than a year ago, an outstanding missionary statesman of the Orient said to me, "The ultimatum of the Protestant Church is 'Unite or die!'" And he continued, "Upon China the impression of Protestant Christianity is today too largely the impression of division and not of unity."

Not only upon China, but upon the world generally, this is the impression made by Protestant Christianity. Out of it has grown an indifference upon the part of intellectuals and youth that has made of Calvary and Easter an argument rather than a passion and an apologetic rather than a trumpet. In the presence of this growing menace of sectarianism and schism, consider Christianity's great rival faiths.

Christianity's Rival Faiths

Shintoism, from having been for two generations a reverence of ancestors and a patriotism, has become throughout the Japanese Empire a militant and coercive religion. And Shintoism is not divided.

Hinduism, not only in India under the inspiration of the Mahatma Gandhi's spiritual leadership, but in Burma, in Siam and in certain of the Dutch East Indies, challenges Christianity at the very heart of the missionary enterprise, and demands that the making of converts cease. Hinduism is comprehensive, all-inclusive, and it is not divided.

Buddhism has over the world taken unto itself the very equipment of the Protestant Church. The newest of the Tokyo Buddhist temples is not unlike the mother church of Christian Science in Boston. It sings our evangelical hymns, takes over our youth activities and organizes educational programs. It is inclusive, it is one. Buddhism is not divided.

Mohammedanism, a religion that makes of the physical sword the weapon of its spiritual advance, now challenges even the medical program of the Christian church, and has long since threatened, if not denied to the missionary, the right of Christian education. This militant religion, shaking itself free of age-old superstitutions, facing in statesmanlike fashion its devitalizing weaknesses, is today definitely on the march. And it is not divided.

The German Christian movement, so-called; Communism, which is both a religion and a social order; totalitarianism in any form, these are fundamental and prophetic unities.

In the lands of these great new experiments, as well as in the more ancient civilizations of the East, questions have been raised that Protestant schism cannot answer. Always for intellectuals and youth of the soul quest, the traditions that divide us, the mere ecclesiastical values that enamor us, the shibboleths that again and again set us against each other, have nothing save only the spirit of division. But these intellectuals and these youth, indeed all men and women who today seek the more abundant life, want none of our divisions and come presently to despise their spirit.

Voice of Youth

I have in my possession a letter written nearly twenty years ago by a young soldier who, returning from France, completed his seminary course and was sent by his church to a city in a western State, where a new congregation was to be organized.

He remained less than six months and then returned to his parents. In his letter are these sentences:

"They sent me there to build a church on a schism, to take advantage of strife in a sister congregation. They sought to capitalize my war record and my wounds for that. I am done. I am in real estate with my father. It is better to divide and subdivide lots than to serve in a divided church."

Christian Endeavorers, this is the voice of youth. Not that youth is always as articulate as was my friend; but there is youthful indifference growing over America and around the world that is not good for society, that is not good for the church, that breaks the heart of Christ, and that, if it continues, will thwart His will in the lives of young men and young women.

In the presence of world crises, in the presence of intimated disaster for our own organizational program and life, in the face of Christ's command and with the passion of His prayer and purpose upon us, what are we going to do about it? Should we discontinue our support of denominational programs? Should we withdraw our service and our money from the churches of our Christian faith?

No! Let there be no misunderstanding here. No! I say! Already we have added too little and withdrawn too much. There can be no unity, spiritual or otherwise, without units. By starving the churches and their far-flung enterprises we would only defeat Christ's purpose and His plan.

What then is to be done?

The Record of Achievement

First of all, thank God for all that is being done. Thank God for progress being made, progress at home and progress overseas. I would have been blind had I not seen the foreign missionary enterprise on the march—valiantly, sacrificially and triumphantly on the march toward a vitalized and a world-vitalizing Christian unity. The glory of the whole Christian enterprise today is in such united projects as the Christian Colleges of China, India and Japan, and the steadily strengthening indigenous Christian churches of the Oriental world.

Nor are we unaware of progress at home. Within a generation the number of united churches in America has grown from a few isolated instances to more than sixteen hundred. In the first three decades of this century more than a score of churches, embracing at least half the total Protestant constituency in the United States, have entered into and continued in, a federated relationship. This body is known as the Federal Council of the Churches of Christ in America. Similar federations have been established in England, France, Holland, Germany and other lands.

Almost startling progress has been made in organic union in America. Eleven mergers have been completed in the last thirty years. In Canada, the Presbyterian, the Methodist and the Congregational Churches have constituted the United Church of Canada. In England, the three Methodist bodies have been consolidated into one. In Scotland, a reunion of the Church of Scotland and the United Free Church has been consummated. Even as I speak, three great bodies of Methodism are perfecting organic union, and surely we may pray for the more complete understanding and unity of all others of this great family.

Inclusive Unity

But the eventual unity of Protestantism, and the only final and effective unity— that unity short of which I believe evangelical Protestantism is today almost if not quite "the most defenseless thing in the world"—must be inclusive and not exclusive. It is unity so comprehensive and complete that it would include us all. It would make possible and practical a world program in which would be preserved and honored every vital principle, every worthy tradition of the several parts.

Dr. E. Stanley Jones in his address, "The Next Great Step—Unite," said concerning the doctrinal basis on which this inclusive unity might be founded:

"I would suggest that the basis be simple—as simple and yet as profound as Christ made it. He founded His church on Peter's confession that He was the Christ, the Son of the living God. That is the rock upon which it is founded. That is the rock beneath us all."

It was this confession of faith that made possible the great Preaching Mission of last year, which is being continued—a mission that is perhaps the greatest single contribution of uniting Protestantism in North America.

Any group or church that accepts and offers this confession could be, should be, at one and in united service with all other groups of like confession. And definite as it is, it is "sufficiently indefinite to give freedom for all marginal differences." Here is the spirit and very genius of Christian Endeavor itself. Here the Christian Endeavor movement may render significant service throughout America and over the whole world.

Common Tasks

But anticipating such an organic union and long before it can be completed, we must find and develop common tasks. In great cities and in rural communities we must unite upon projects. Everywhere at home and abroad we must enlist the support of Protestant Christians—not in terms of their divisions but by the test of their common faith and in the spirit of Christ's prayer. Nor let us ever forget that while "it is the letter that killeth," always it is "the spirit maketh alive." It is the spirit that in the presence of these major world disasters offers us a path of hope toward destiny and power, for it is the spirit that leads us straight to Jesus Christ Himself.

And whatever else Christ left behind Him on Olivet, He did leave one company, not one hundred, less or more. Surely there is no debate among us on the proposition that He desires the members of that company to be as one. The Christian church is an institution at once human and divine. As such, today it may be as weak as man, but eventually it is as powerful as God and through it at last "He shall reign where'er the sun doth his successive journeys run."

The Sufficient Christ

The world rocks. The Protestant Church, challenged by the occasion, if not "defenseless" is at least inadequate, and Jesus Christ Himself He alone—is sufficient.

Jesus Christ has, Jesus Christ is, the only solution for the world's problem. And He is so complete and powerful, He Himself is so entirely adequate that eventually, in spite of all our divisions, in spite of all our failures, He will complete the salvation of the world. In Him is our unity. Color, language, race, nations, and denominations divide us. With bitterness in our divisions we contend against each other unto death. But all colors, all races, all tongues, all nations and all denominations, are at last of the one blood of His eternal covenant.

Here and nowhere else is the true prophecy for the consummation of His prayer, for as more and more we center our gaze upon Him, we shall find ourselves withdrawn from the littleness that divides us.

Another has said: "The world as we know it is headed straight for self-destruction and moving fast." Can anything save it? Well, the answer to be effective must be convincing and prompt.

Good, But Not Enough

What of the answer, "Economic Justice"? Surely economic injustice and selfish nationalism are a folly. Surely we must study the economic causes of armed conflict and then eventually decide that only a world state to administer world affairs is adequate to maintain the world peace. Here the unity of the peace-makers, rather than their uniformity, is required. Here the church and all religions may play an increasing part in a comprehensive study of inter-racial and economic conditions that make for suspicion and fear and that invite armed conflict whenever the strong exploit the weak or when justice fails.

But the answer of economic justice inter-racially applied and of world peace without a higher purpose, clearly is outmoded and inadequate. These of themselves are cold, while nationalism and war are passions. Only a mightier passion can overthrow both selfish nationalism and armed conflict. Justice itself may be as cold as steel and as brutal as mob action. "Man cannot live by bread alone," though he cannot exist without it. Patriotism is not enough and freedom itself may become brutal and brutalizing license.

Education is good, but it is not enough. Laboratories of science have trapped disease germs to destroy them or to release them upon hapless communities. Knowledge can become as ruthless as wings over Spain and as horrible as poison gas.

Ethics are good, but they are not enough. The Orient has been immersed in ethics for five millenniums, but these have achieved little more than a callous disregard for individual life and a stoical silence in the presence of human suffering.

Political action may be good, but it is not enough. Man cannot be legislated into self-respect or made intrinsically worthy by law. Politics offer an equal opportunity for the sinister demagogue and the unselfish captain of the state. Character cannot be achieved by a fiat of government; and without character in the citizen, the state itself, however free in form, will be destroyed by dry-rot from within.

What, then, is the answer?

Are we to disregard, or consider and then dismiss, economic and social justice, peace action, education, a revival in ethical standards, and government in its own field?

Certainly not, certainly not, unless we are either designing persons or social and moral defeatists. But the ultimate answer to the questions here raised is not the answer of economics nor of education nor of ethics nor of government.

Survey the Cross

Dr. Samuel M. Zwemer once said, "We are having all sorts of surveys today. There is good, I am sure, in all of them. But there is one survey that we do not make often enough—the survey of the Cross, the Cross on which the Prince of Glory died."

Christian Endeavorers, *the* answer is the Cross.

Fundamentally, a "world headed straight for self-destruction" may have many needs, but is confronted by one and only one imperative—power sufficient to turn it around! For this achievement there is only one formula, the formula that is the Cross. "Believe on the Lord Jesus Christ and thou shalt be saved and thy house," were the words of Paul to the jailer of Philippi who was in the act of destroying himself. There are no other words than these adequate for a "world headed straight for self-destruction."

Nor is this belief a mere intellectual affirmation. It is revolution. It is a new man and a new woman. It is the regeneration of the individual, of individual practice and of society itself. It is the New Birth, a birth as mysterious as the coming of a new life into the world and *more* profound.

This is the Gospel of the Son of God, not a divided Gospel, the Gospel whole. There is no "personal Gospel." There is no "social Gospel." The Gospel is one. It cannot be divided. Justification is by faith; faith without works is dead. Here are the halves of the Gospel's perfect whole. Here, though men may strive, they strive in vain. It is the Gospel whole—personal first and social always. Today the old-time sense of individual sin grows within the hearts of men. A madhouse world has made this inevitable. But with this sense of individual sin has risen a new tide, a tide of mighty volume, "a sense of corporate guilt."

Nothing short of a new society, a community life in which privilege is shared as well as the bare necessities of existence—nothing short of the plan of Jesus for a society of man in the Fatherhood of God—will prove sufficient. But this new world comes only through new world-builders, new men and new women; and for such a task men and women become adequate only through personal redemption.

Here is an adventure and triumph greater than the offering of any dictator. About its universal order, far-visioning Christian statesmen are establishing tasks and programs that comprehend every human hunger, every physical, intellectual, moral and spiritual quest. In these, and not with Communism nor Fascism, in these and with Him is the "Forward, March!" of the Twentieth Century.

Today Youth's most alluring leadership is not with Hitler or Stalin, with Mussolini or Kemal, or with the Emperor—it is with Jesus Christ. Over the world youth marches, marches at the call of personalities, rather than because of program or ideals. Forever it is the passion for a person that challenges young men and women to sacrifice and achievement. Jesus Jesus Christ alone, has an attractiveness that for young men and young women transcends the attractiveness of the dictators. When He is revealed and released, He wins over all. With Him, and with no other, the Christian Church—with Him and with no other, Protestant Christianity may build in the hearts of men, through all human relationships and over all the nations, the Kingdom of Heaven.

Sunday Evening

"The Glory of the Crisis," by Rev. Louis H. Evans, D.D. Dr. Evans is the pastor of the Third Presbyterian Church of Pittsburgh, Pa. His success with young people has been a marked characteristic of each of his pastorates. In addition he stands high in his denomination, being chairman of the Board of National Missions.

"The Glory of the Crisis"

SINCE a lad I have had a sneaking admiration for pirates. It has lain solely in the fact that in recruiting crews they made men to understand that between them and booty, bounty, jewels and gold lay possible storms, hunger, wounds and pain. They recruited men to live dangerously. Garibaldi did the same thing in challenging men to build with him an Empire—he challenged men to live dangerously for a great cause. Admiral Byrd's men were reminded, or they knew without being reminded, that between them and their goal lay possible blizzards, ice, isolation, hunger, and hardship. He recruited men who loved to live dangerously.

I have an open and illimitable admiration for Christ. He recruited men with these hard promises, "Ye shall be hated of all men for my name's sake; they that kill you will think they do God a service. I send you forth as sheep in the midst of wolves." He did not promise them full dinner pails, higher wages, shorter hours, employment, and fewer taxes. He offered them the possibility of losing everything but their own souls. He dared men to dangerous living!

Beware of bargain hunting in religion! Only eternal life is free and Christ paid for that with His life, and with that life there come obligations that grow out of it. Christ too challenges youth to dangerous living. I love Christ because it costs too much to give Him up; but also because it costs a great deal to keep Him! The glory of the church is youth who live dangerously. Do you want to?

The glory for which you are asked to live dangerously is not the glory of piratical bounty, of extending the borders of an empire, but the glory of Christ and the glory of seeing a Christ-like world. You are interested in that, of course. No aim of life is quite so soulless as that expressed by a young college man in these words. "My own welfare and happiness are all that I deem worth a hoot I intend to use my wit to squeeze out the world's rich jocose juices and go swimming in them!"

Over against that selfish aim place this, "This is my Father's world, the battle is not done; Jesus who died shall be satisfied, and Heaven and earth be one." That is the glory for which we would live dangerously.

There is much to do. Mr. Ickes said that his generation "had made a mess of things." While we do not scorn our father's accomplishments, we may do no better ourselves. We may do better if we will. They have left us with great problems unsolved—war, intemperance, class hatred, unrest, a broken Sabbath, an unevangelized world, in part.

But Christ is the hope of glory. There is no need of debating this matter. Where Christ has been left out of our experiments we have failed ignobly. In Russia there are now 2,000 divorces for every 3,700 marriages. The Registry of Leningrad records two and a half years as its average length of marriage.

As to war, God will have to change the hearts of men before we bring wars to cease. Men still love war! They hated typhus, typhoid fever, slavery, yellow fever, and they did away with them. If men hated war they would have done away with that long ago. Men still love war.

As one writer said, "There is nothing in the world that can match war for popularity. It is the greatest circus in the world. It combines all the excitement of a bull fight, a revival, a train wreck and a lynching. The hearts of men are thrown into a cocktail shaker. Old men make speeches and hunt spies. Old gals knit socks and dream of winning handsome generals. New and better jobs and more profit. War is the dizziest, gaudiest, grandest, damnedest thing that the human mind can imagine."

Until we make men hate war in their hearts, there is no hope for peace. This is where religion, God, and Christ come in.

The trouble with the business is that we have left God out. All program and no prayer, all work and no worship, revenue more than righteousness, and human cleverness and law in place of God and His guidance.

As the Pittsburgh business man said, "Too long, O God, we have trusted in the gods of commerce and of gold and now these gods have failed us. We have met much and planned much, but we have not been silent to listen to Thy voice. We became wise in our own conceits. And now we are filled with doubt and dread and fear of disaster. I for one want to come back to the faith of my boyhood days. God, come and share this desk with me and help me run this business for Thy glory. Help me to be Thy man again, unashamed and unafraid. Amen."

We need Christ for these crises!

Bernard Shaw said, "I am ready to admit that after contemplating the misery of the world and human nature for more than sixty years, I see no way out of the world's misery but the way that would have been found by Christ's will if He had undertaken the work of a modern practical statesman." But that is what Christ expects us to do—put His teachings into practice courageously!

Some may say, "We have tried Christ for two thousand years." We have not tried Christ for twenty minutes—all of society, all of government, all of the people. What we need today is not so much more leaders—but more followers, more men to follow Christ and the sermon on the mount and dare to try it and live it and work it!

"Those Ushers Made a very Attractive Picture."

Christ in you is the hope of glory. Christianity is a religion of experience. You cannot change a nation until you change individuals. When Christ means something real to you, then you may pass Him on to the world, not until then. Animals come before zoology—the latter is but the outgrowth of our experience with animals. Christ comes before theology, so your creed is simply the expression of what you have found Christ to mean. Your belief is no substitute for experience. Handel's Messiah is useless unless you find someone to sing and play it. What if Christ is Life, if there is no one to live Him? What if Christ be Light if we are not candlesticks to hold aloft that light? It is Christ in YOU, not in your preacher, your leader, your Congress, that is the hope of glory.

These ideals take courage. "They followed after Him into Jerusalem and they were sore afraid." I do not wonder. It takes courage to follow the marks of His wounded feet. It cost a Theban Legion their six thousand heads to refuse to go on a bloody expedition of greed for Caesar. It cost Lincoln his life to sign the proclamation that set a race free. It has cost men their positions to stand for conscience in business. It cost Telemachus his life in the arena at Rome to stop the bloody gladiatorial contests, when stepping between two gladiators, having leaped into the arena, he cried, "In the name of Jesus Christ, stop this bloody business!" And it may cost you, young people, a great deal to change things in this crisis.

You will need confidence also. Christ in you is hope enough for glory. You have Christ as your companion, living, real, practical, ever-present. Caesar had a greater army than Christ, but Caesar is dead now. Socrates had more followers than Christ in his day but not now; the subtleties of the Socratic mind rest upon a memory. The Communists embalm the body of Lenin and well-nigh worship it. But when the embalming fluids no longer can do their work—then what? Men cannot live on a memory or a ghost. Christ lives today—He walks with men, talks with men, helps men, guides men. He is the living Comrade of countless lives.

A lad lost in London asked the way home. Said the policeman, "Two squares to the right, lad, then cross a bridge, go two squares to the left, then go over a hill, stop there and inquire again." By this time the lad was confused. As he stood there bewildered and afraid a kindly man came up to him and throwing his warm cloak over the lad's shoulders, said, "Come, lad, I will show you the way." The lad walked along, his little hand clasped in the larger one. That is Christ.

The Euthenist tells us to be beautiful, but not how. The scientist informs us, the psychologist instructs us, the ethical teacher commands us, but Christ *helps* us. "Christ keepeth him and the Evil One toucheth him not." That is our confidence, that in the crisis of personal temptation Christ will be sufficient for the test. It is Christ in you, not yourself. Not self-control—Christ-control. The man who at Niagara knows that by pulling a lever he releases a half million horse-power is neither proud nor arrogant for this, knowing the power is not in him but in Niagara. He has but the use of that power. It is Christ in us who gives power. He can keep us from "going to pieces."

The hope of glory. Do you hope for it—really want it—the glory of victory for yourself and the world? A Communist said to a group of students on a college campus some time ago, "We Communists have the one and only cure for the world's ills."

One interrupted with the question, "Hasn't the church anything to offer?"

He replied, "Yes, the church people could do what we are doing if it could get enough people soundly converted so that they would go out and put the principles of Christ into effect. But I have no hope that they ever will. They are too indifferent or too lazy or blind or ignorant or selfish. It looks as if they do not greatly care."

Will you young people let him say that without a challenge? Will you throw that back in his teeth again? *You don't care?* Are you too lazy, too afraid to put the principles of Christ into action?

We do not care to do some of the things the Communist suggests we do. But what is Christlike, what is right? Do we want the glory and the pain of that?

I beg to remind him that the arenas of Rome were stained with blood of men and women who cared, that hundreds of thousands of young people died in the Crusades and left their bones on desert sands to capture a land for Christ. Would we do it again with the better weapons of love? Ten thousand fists went up in a salute to Jesus Christ at the Philadelphia Convention two years ago, saying, "We Choose Christ!" If half those young people meant it, they can and will tear this world loose from sin and wrong and give it back again to Jesus Christ. Do we want the glory for Himself and for ourselves with all its scars and pain?

The way is hard, but it is a glorious way and we have a glorious Commander. Let us rededicate our lives to this task, to this crisis. Should He at any hour look down upon us and ask us how the warfare progresses, may we be able to give back to Him these words of our desire?

> "More than half beaten but fearless
> Here in the lull of this fight;
> With hardship and foes all about me,
> God, give me the strength to do right!
> With head all bowed down and bloody,
> God of this fighting clan;
> Lifting my fists I implore Thee,
> Give me the heart of a man!"

Christ in you is the glory of the crisis!

MONDAY EVENING

"The Technique of Spiritual Power," by Rev. Norman Vincent Peale, Ph.D. Dr. Peale is pastor of the Marble Collegiate Church, New York City, where he succeeded Dr. Poling.

"The Technique of Spiritual Power"

OUR generation, expert in technological power, is strangely inexpert in spiritual power. Adept in dealing with the natural sciences we are for the most part novices in handling the important science of spiritual forces. We have learned to draw power out of the universe in a thousand different ways. We drew power out for wireless and radio communication. We drew power out to operate our great turbines and machinery. Having tapped this power for use in so many practical ways, it should convince us that other and greater power lies waiting for our benefit. Accomplishments in the field of natural power, notable as they are, indubitably are but forerunners of greater achievements yet to be realized.

An eminent scientist of the General Electric Company recently declared, 'Each new item of our electrical past has opened still more fertile areas in the unknown. We can never reach a limit of discovery while we work." If it is true that further power lies waiting in the realm of electro-mechanics, it throws into relief the possibility that there are other areas than mechanics where even greater power may lie. The story of mechanical and electrical invention is a bright, even amazing, page in man's history. Those who pioneer in the discovery of spiritual power, however, may ultimately be marked as greater scientists and nobler benefactors than those who have operated in the field of materialistic science. No man can logically assume that the power utilized by the natural sciences is the only manifestation of power extant in the universe. The romance of exploring in the field of spiritual power holds the possibility of being one of the most alluring adventures of our age.

If it is possible for a man to reach out into the universe and draw down power to light our cities and homes, why can we not reach out into the same universe and draw out spiritual power to illuminate this world, to drive away the dark shadows of fear, prejudice, war, and economic troubles? Is there not resident in the universe another light that will shine into the darkened corners of a man's mind and illuminate his soul? I can not agree to the assumption that the Creator made a power to light up a room and failed to make a power to light up a man. To discover this kind of power demands no scientific genius, like Edison, but simple, honorable spiritually surrendered men willing to pay the cost.

Our generation desperately needs this form of power. We have heretofore put a naïve faith in sophisticated philosophies and bright machinery, but they have generally failed us. This broken, battered, and disillusioned world finds little strength or healing in ideas and points of view once so brightly, even jauntily, cherished. Thoughtful men are realizing that we have lost contact with the genuine sources of power and that a generation which felt itself to be in all ways adequate to its own needs is all but sterile in the face of overwhelming difficulties. We must once again tap that ancient and mystic power which in times past has saved men and nations.

Our age must discover the impotency of many of its philosophies, complacent schemes, and machineries, and turn again to that deeper force we call the power of God.

What society needs, the individual man also requires. The problem of living with oneself is for most people the really difficult fact of life. Dwight L. Moody was once asked to name the man who had caused him more trouble than any other man he had ever met. Unhesitatingly and quickly he replied, "The man's name is Dwight L. Moody."

I can say the same about Norman Vincent Peale. In fact, he gets on my nerves, for he is all too ready to do the things I do not want him to do, and he easily fails to do the things I do want him to do! Every honest man will make the same admission about himself. A chief need of every individual is to find a power or force by which he can control himself and handle effectively the problems and burdens life lays upon him. To realize that there is available for him a spiritual power which will carry his life forward in a manner as different as the motorcar from the oxcart should awaken him to the point of seizing the romance of spiritual power. The problem for society and the individual is to learn how to secure and use this power.

Here is where the church enters the picture. Many people have a faulty conception of the church. They see it as a dull, often lifeless, institution. Some time ago I went through Schenectady, New York, and my train passed the General Electric plant, where they generate and deal in power. I chanced to see not far away an old church which had apparently fallen into some disuse. It had a look of resigned hopelessness and defeatism about it. It occurred to me then that essentially the function of the church is that of the General Electric Company—to release power. But the former was content, it seemed, to mumble prayers and recite creeds. It had forgotten its purpose, which is to release for the individual and society the spiritual power inherent in the world and freely offered to those who want it and will take it. It did that in its early days. Christianity then obviously possessed power. It was an overwhelming sensation in every community into which it came. In tragically few places is it a sensation today. Too often it seems to be old, dead stuff, which makes little or no impression on the community life.

The power within Christianity, however, is not dead. It is merely impeded in its flow by hollow forms and as empty formalists, but like rivers when the spring freshets come, again and again in human history it has broken its dams and overflowed with refreshing vitality into the life of the world.

That flood, I believe, is again on the way. Religious leaders are learning that as the church recognizes its function to be the teaching of the simple and practical technique of spiritual power to day-by-day men and women it is opening the way for a new chapter in the romance of the spirit. The church has been stung by the fact pointed out by such men as Dr. C. G. Jung, the noted psychologist, that today in ever-increasing numbers harassed men turn to the physician rather than to the minister for mental and spiritual relief.

In the wholly worth-while attempt to create a new social order the church has neglected with tragic frequency the human beings who make up that same social order and who have been hard put to it to get a handout of spiritual bread by which to live with some degree of strength and courage in the social order that is. Real Christianity is that to which baffled, frustrated people should be able to turn as thirsty men to a deep, cool spring where invigorating waters flow.

Our fathers knew the art of spiritual power. They harnessed it to their lives and their society. One of the supreme needs of this generation is a concrete, simple, workable technique of the spiritual life. People must not only be told they should pray but also be taught how to pray. If they are told that God will help them, they must also know in a practical sense just how to receive that aid. In a word, we need to relearn the definite procedure for releasing spiritual vitality in the individual and in society. How is it to be done?

Let us say, first of all, that formal belief in religion or mere observance of its forms yields little practical aid, but that personal surrender taps overflowing reservoirs of spiritual power. A glance at the history of religion and its effect on men illustrates what I have in mind. Christ, as he neared the end of His career on earth, was on a hilltop with His disciples. In His years of association He had become well acquainted with these men, realizing their weakness and knowing their strength. They were simple Galilean peasants, ordinary run-of-the-mill fellows. Some were fishermen, one was a tax-gatherer, and none of them had any particular claim to distinction. Looking at them, the Master said an apparently impossible thing: "Ye shall receive power after the Holy Spirit has come upon you." In current speech that was to say: "You men are to be endowed with amazing power, the like of which you never dreamed, when God's abiding Spirit is received into your hearts." They were simple enough to believe that He knew whereof He spoke. They were naïve enough to take Him at His word, and with what a result!

The Bible, with simple eloquence tells us that they went out and turned the world upside down. They changed the stream of history; they inspired the rewriting of the philosophies of the world; they scrambled the political map for generations yet to be; they toppled autocrats off the thrones of great empires; they destroyed those empires; they established democracy; they have kept the world in ferment until now, and will continue to do so until the Kingdom comes. They moved forward with a power that was irresistible, these simple men.

Read the story of their conquest of Athens, the intellectual capital of the ancient world. These men had no learning, but they moved up against Athens, where they found the great, towering intellects and a cultural life, imperious and haughty. These thinkers of Athens examined with speculative curiosity and intellectual dilettantism every new idea, but nothing had ever laid hold of their wills or changed their lives until the Christians came with an intellectual and spiritual force that cut through to the very heart of their idle skepticism.

These plain peasants marched up to the Acropolis and in one of the most amazing romances of history captured in the name of Christ the intellectual citadel of their age. How is it to be explained? On one basis only—they had tapped the secret of a power that nothing could stop. They were never more than a small fraction of the great population of the East. They were people from the lower stratum of society. They had no money, no education, no social standing, no prestige—in short, no reason at all for their amazing accomplishments except the supreme one, that they had discovered the technique of an all-conquering power.

So it has been throughout all history. When the moral and spiritual life of the world had fallen to a low ebb, when society had become corrupt and the church was innocuous, there lived in the beautiful city of Assisi, down among the Umbrian Hills, a gay youth by the name of Francis. He lived for pleasure and was crowned by his companions King of the Revels. But he was not satisfied with his life, and one day in a wayside shrine he stopped for rest, little realizing the wonder about to take place. He came as most people come to the church, not expecting anything to happen. The priest was idly and indifferently reading over the words of the Scriptures when the miracle happened—or was it a miracle? The cold print often thought to be lifeless began to glow. It became incandescent and fire leaped from it into the heart of Francis and he was transformed. He moved out into the roadways of Italy and into the streets of crowded cities, preaching with such winsome beauty and such effectiveness that he transformed his age, and the fragrance of his life lingers to this very day.

What had happened? He too had discovered the secret found by the disciples twelve centuries before and had become the awestruck possessor of mighty spiritual power.

Again, in the eighteenth century the saddest days in her history had fallen upon England. It was the period of Walpole, in which English morals and religion were all but prostrate. Multitudes were living in degradation. Society for the most part was licentious and impure; politics was corrupt. Even the clergy were, many of them, men of unworthy life, and the churches, half-heartedly supported, were shorn of spiritual influence. Into this situation, like a current of fresh air from sunlit mountain peaks, appeared one, John Wesley, and it came about in this way:

One night this young preacher, who possessed a cold, ethical philosophy but no power other than that bequeathed by a brilliant intellect and noble heritage, went into a meeting in Aldersgate Street. Here, as in the case of Francis, a man was reading the Scriptures. Again the cold print grew warm; it began to glow until it became incandescent with a white heat and power leaped from the Book into the heart of Wesley, who went out and preached with such eloquence and persuasion that multitudes were changed. Green, the historian of the British people, declared that more was accomplished for England under the preaching of the Wesleys than all the victories won on land or sea by the elder Pitt. What had happened? Wesley, in the eighteenth century, like Francis and the disciples, had discovered the technique of spiritual power.

How can the individual secure this spiritual power? In the releasing of spiritual power the removal of a subtle blockade to a free flow of that power is important. This has to do with the matter of ethical and moral obstructions. It is at this point that thoughtful men are realizing that the trouble with our age may not be a lack of intellectual brilliance but, rather, moral deficiency. Dr. Alexis Carrel, in "Man, the Unknown," has an unforgettable passage:

"Despite the immense hopes which humanity has placed in modern civilization, such a civilization has failed in developing men of sufficient intelligence and audacity to guide it along the dangerous road on which it is stumbling. Human beings have not grown so rapidly as the institutions sprung from their brains. It is chiefly the intellectual and moral deficiencies of the political leaders, and their ignorance, which endanger modern nations."

For some strange reason written into the constitution of the universe the power of God in spiritual form cannot in any abundance flow past the evil in men's lives. To the degree to which men generally seek and receive forgiveness and live a cleansed moral life does spiritual power operate in their affairs. When men are crooked, their affairs will be crooked, for obviously they cannot see straight.

"As a man thinketh in his heart, so is he," is a truism for society as well as for the individual.

Spiritual power is released by faith in and surrender to God. These two terms are closely related. Because they are old religious terms and therefore perhaps not clear to the average man they need interpretation. By faith we do not mean intellectual assent to a prescribed doctrine or creed. Rather do we refer to a childlike trust in and dependence upon God in a manner similar to the attitude a child would have toward a loving father. Surrender is predicated on faith but perhaps goes a step further. It has a double meaning. First, to surrender is to take something out of your life, to give it up, to part with it. Obviously, it means to give up sin of any kind or degree, gross sins of the flesh manifestly, but also the more subtle sins of the disposition. Many so-called Christians might not inappropriately be termed "segment Christians," which is to say that they have been changed or converted only in certain segments of their nature. They may have given nine-tenths of their lives to God's direction but one-tenth may still belong to a lower order. Perhaps a certain clergyman may fall under this classification. When asked how his church was doing, he glumly replied, "Not so well," and then hastened to add, "but the Baptists aren't doing any better." The fact that he said it at all, to say nothing of the satisfaction implied, would indicate that at least a segment of his life needed to be surrendered or have something more taken out of it.

Secondly, surrender means to put something into your life, and the thing to put in is faith, the kind of faith by which one can truly rest on God. Great power is available to the person who learns to trust God completely, that is, to utterly rest his life with all of its problems and burdens on God.

TUESDAY EVENING

Extracts from the address of Dr. Frederick W. Norwood, of London, England:

The most remorseful person is not the great sinner, it is he who has sinned just once and cannot forgive himself. God's forgiveness is spiritual and absolute but it doesn't alter the chain of events or prevent the harvest of the seed sown. God does not wipe out sin with a damp cloth; the forgiven one must face the consequences.

We think too much of the meekness of Christ. There is violence about Christ even yet. All through the ages He has done extraordinary things to people—turned them upside down. He turned the respectable Pharisee Saul into a humble seeker of the lost with the compassion of Christ.

I hope the days will come when there will be something of the violence of Christ manifested in the church. A disturbing experience of Christ would make the church not the most respectable of companies but the most vital and thrilling of companies.

The worst customs are those by which men seek to bring Jesus Christ into alignment with themselves. Religion has done that all too often. Intolerance has been justified in the name of Christ; slavery was; war and economic injustice are still so justified. But Christ spreads the infection of an unquiet spirit and again and again men have rediscovered power in Him to break through their customs into larger liberty and deeper life.

Extracts from the address of Bishop L. Westinghouse Kyles, of North Carolina:

You will not be surprised when I tell you that so far as my racial group is concerned, this question of race relations is the touchstone of American Christianity. Let me remind you of a few items in the dark catalogue of race relations in America:

In the matter of education there yet remain far too many cases of gross inequality of opportunity for the Negro, and shameful injustice in the distribution of school funds   In hundreds of counties the proportion runs as high as ten to one, and in some, twenty to one, in favor of white children.

There is no reason why an alleged criminal should not be given a fair trial by due process of law   The entire machinery of the court is in the hands of the dominant race, and a Negro who was proven guilty would not have the slightest chance to escape the penalty of the law. The appalling thing about lynching is that many who compose the mobs that indulge in these brutal orgies are professedly Christian people.

If American Christianity is inadequate to make the necessary adjustments in race relations, how shall we meet the crisis in the Far East and on what grounds are we justified in sending missionaries to preach a gospel that has proven inadequate for our needs?

Brief statements worth pondering:

"We should show by our works that Christians can labor together even while they are in different denominations."

—*Dr. Harry Thomas Stock*

"Christianity will work in any political system *on its own terms.*"

—*Dr. Albert J. Anthony*

"The greatest fault of American youth is that they are soft. They need disciplined minds, manners, characters.   . .

"It makes no difference what kind of program is developed for young people if ultimately they have to go to war."

—*Dr. Homer P. Rainey*

"The people of India *are* coming to accept the Christian religion. Throngs are coming. We cannot take them in as fast as they come. They must be taught properly first, or there will be as many unregenerate church members in India as there are at home!"

—*Dr. Norma P. Dunning*

VII

Questions Asked and Answered in the Young People's Radio Conference

HERE are just a few samples of the questions asked by young people and answered by Dr. Poling during the Young People's Radio Conference held each day during the Grand Rapids Convention from noon until twelve-thirty.

Q. *What is the question that young people have asked you more frequently than any other?*

A. I speak out of years of experience. I find that ninety-nine out of every one hundred young people ask the same question. They ask it in their own words but it is the same. From all parts of the world comes the question, "What must I do to make my life count? What kind of books should I read? What college shall I go to? Where should I put my life to make it count for the most?"

Q. *What is the creed of Christian Endeavor? Is it the Apostles' Creed?*

A. The creed of Christian Endeavor is the creed of your particular church. Christian Endeavor does not have a creed. You owe your allegiance first to God, then to the church of which you are a part. In this large organization we include mighty groups, which do not have a creed. Our unity is a unity of fellowship, unity in Christ.

Q. *Who named Christian Endeavor?*

A. Francis E. Clark.

Q. *Why should I go to church when so many church members are hypocrites?*

A. The church is not an institution to give to us only. The church needs us as much as we need it. We human beings fail in our humanity. The church needs your vital living to confound hypocrites.

You do not discard dollar bills because there are counterfeits.

Q. *Where can we get information about tobacco?*

A. From the Life Extension Institute. New York City, or the Woman's Christian Temperance Union, Evanston, Illinois.

Q. *How can we be loyal to our denomination and to Christian Endeavor?*

A. The most loyal members of Christian Endeavor are the most loyal members of the church. In my own church the Christian Endeavor Society has worked to increase by thousands of dollars the gifts of the young people to our denominational Board of Foreign Missions.

75

Q. *Was Prohibition a success?*

A. Prohibition was not an automatic machine, as we thought of it, but it was an opportunity. There are permissive laws and mandatory laws. Prohibition was a permissive law. It was the refusal of the privileged classes to give up liquor which started the break-down of Prohibition—the "Rolls-Royce Rebellion."

Q. *What do you think of Repeal?*

A. Repeal has succeeded in failing to do every single thing it promised to do. Before Prohibition there were two hundred thousand saloons. Today there are four hundred seventy-three thousand liquor sales places, many of them infinitely worse than saloons. One of the worst features is the employment of young women as barmaids.

MOTHER ENDEAVOR CLARK GREETS THE YOUNGEST DELEGATE TO THE JUNIOR
CONVENTION,—RUTH ELEANOR VER MULEN, THE SIX-YEAR-OLD
DAUGHTER OF A GRAND RAPIDS PHYSICIAN

General Committee

1. George Veldman, *General Chairman;*
2. Lester C. Doerr, *Associate Chairman;*
3. Lawrence D. Beukema, *Vice-Chairman;*
4. Russell J.Boyle, *Vice-Chairman;* 5. Fred P. Geib, *Vice-Chairman;* 6. H. Fred Oltman, *Vice-Chairman;* 7. Frank V. Smith, *Vice-Chairman;* 8. Mrs. M. J. Van Ess, *Secretary;* 9. Clifford Buchanan, *Treasurer;* 10. Ernest S. Marks, *State Secretary;* 11. Carroll M. Wright, *National Secretary;* 12. Carroll Herlein, *President G. R. Union;* 13. Advisory Committee: Leland S. Westerman, *Chairman;* 14. Ministerial Association: Rev. Edward P. Downey, *Chairman.*

—*Photographs through the courtesy and cooperation of the Merrild W. Coulter Studio.*

Holy Communion Service

Sunday, July 11, 8:00 A.M.

"This Do in Remembrance of Me"

Order of Service

PRELUDE

HYMN—"When Morning Gilds the Sky" (standing)

When morning gilds the skies,
My heart awaking cries,
May Jesus Christ be praised!
Alike at work and prayer,
To Jesus I repair,
May Jesus Christ be praised!

Whene'er the sweet church bell
Peals over hill and dell,
May Jesus Christ be praised!
O hark to what it sings,
As joyously it rings,
May Jesus Christ be praised!

In heaven's eternal bliss
The loveliest strain is this,
May Jesus Christ be praised!
Let earth and sea and sky
From depth to height reply,
May Jesus Christ be praised!

Be this, while life is mine,
My canticle divine,
May Jesus Christ be praised!
Be this the eternal song
Through ages all along,
May Jesus Christ be praised!

INVOCATION AND LORD'S PRAYER (in unison, standing)

CHORALE

RESPONSIVE LESSON—Psalm 103

Bless the Lord, O my soul: and all that is within me, bless his holy name.

Bless the Lord, O my soul; and forget not all his benefits:

Who forgiveth all thine iniquities; who healeth all thy diseases;

Who redeemeth thy life from destruction; who crowneth thee with loving-kindness and tender mercies;

Who satisfieth thy mouth with good things: so that thy youth is renewed like the eagle's.

The Lord executeth righteousness and judgment: for all that are oppressed.

He made known his ways unto Moses: his acts unto the children of Israel.

The Lord is merciful and gracious: slow to anger, and plenteous in mercy.

He will not always chide: neither will he keep his anger forever.

He hath not dealt with us after our sins: nor rewarded us according to our iniquities.

For as the heaven is high above the earth: so great is his mercy toward them that fear him.

As far as the east is from the west: so far hath he removed our transgressions from us.

Like as a father pitieth his children: so the Lord pitieth them that fear him.

For he knoweth our frame: he remembereth that we are dust.

As for man, his days are as grass: as a flower of the field, so he flourisheth.

For the wind passeth over it, and it is gone: and the place thereof shall know it no more.

But the mercy of the Lord is from everlasting to everlasting upon them that fear him: and his righteousness unto children's children;

To such as keep his covenant: and to those that remember his commandments to do them.

The Lord hath prepared his throne in the heavens: and his kingdom ruleth over all.

Bless the Lord, ye his angels, that excel in strength: that do his commandments, hearkening unto the voice of his word.

Bless the Lord, all ye his hosts: ye ministers of his, that do his pleasure.

Bless the Lord, all his works in all places of his dominion: bless the Lord, O my soul.

PRAYER

HYMN—"Beneath the Cross of Jesus" (standing)

Beneath the cross of Jesus
I fain would take my stand
The shadow of a mighty rock
Within a weary land;
A home within the wilderness,
A rest upon the way,
From the burning of the noon-tide heat
And the burden of the day.

Upon the cross of Jesus,
Mine eye at times can see
The very dying form of One
Who suffered there for me;
And from my smitten heart with tears
These wonders I confess:
The wonder of His glorious love,
And my unworthiness.

I take, O Cross, thy shadow
For my abiding-place;
I ask no other sunshine than
The sunshine of His face;
Content to let the world go by,
To know no gain nor loss,
My sinful self my only shame,
My glory all the cross.

THE LORD'S SUPPER

THE WORDS OF INSTITUTION

PRAYER OF INSTITUTION (unison)

Most gracious God, the Father of
our Lord Jesus Christ, whose once
offering up of Himself upon the cross
we commemorate before Thee; we
earnestly desire Thy fatherly goodness
to accept this our sacrifice of praise
and Thanksgiving:

And we pray Thee to bless and sanctify with Thy Word and Spirit these
Thine own gifts of Bread and Wine
which we set before Thee, that we may
receive by faith Christ crucified for us,
and so feed upon Him that He may be
made one with us and we with Him.

And here we offer and present unto
Thee ourselves, our souls and bodies,
to be a reasonable, holy and living
sacrifice unto Thee: praying that all
we, who are partakers of this Holy
Communion, may find that in this
place Thou givest peace;

Through Jesus Christ our Lord; to
whom with Thee and the Holy Spirit,
be the glory and the praise, both now
and evermore. Amen.

THE ADMINISTERING OF THE BREAD

THE ADMINISTERING OF THE CUP

PRAYER OF THANKSGIVING AND CONSECRATION (unison)

Almighty God our Heavenly Father,
we thank Thee for this holy hour.
Thou hast brought us to Thy banqueting house and Thy banner over us is
love. We have been refreshed in spirit
by the presence of Thy Son our living
Lord whose victorious death we have
commemorated. We have come from
all the corners of our nation and from
many churches and homes but we are
all one in Him. We thank Thee for
our precious fellowship in Him and
with each other. As we go upon our
way we would consecrate ourselves
anew to the service of our fellow men in
Jesus' name. We would go forth under
the sign of His Cross to fight the good
fight of faith and to endure to the end.
May Thy kingdom of righteousness,
goodwill and peace come among all
men. May all injustice and evil be
overthrown Send us forth in the
power of Thy Holy Spirit to do even
"greater things than these" according
to our Master's promise, who first
chose us, and whom we have chosen
in loving obedience. And to Thee,
Father, Son and Holy Ghost, one God,
will we ascribe everlasting praise,
world without end. Amen.

HYMN—"O Jesus I Have Promised" (standing)

O Jesus, I have promised
To serve Thee to the end;
Be Thou forever near me,
My Master and my Friend;

I shall not fear the battle
 If Thou art by my side.
Nor wander from the pathway
 If Thou wilt be my Guide.

O let me feel Thee near me,
 The world is ever near;
I see the sights that dazzle,
 The tempting sounds I hear;
My foes are ever near me,
 Around me and within;
But Jesus, draw Thou nearer,
 And shield my soul from sin.

O Jesus. Thou hast promised
 To all who follow Thee,
That where Thou art in glory
 There shall Thy servant be;
And, Jesus, I have promised
 To serve Thee to the end;
O give me grace to follow,
 My Master and my Friend

BENEDICTION AND MIZPAH
(unison)

Mother Clark's Morning Prayer Poem

"Lord, give me strength, I pray,
 To live my life this day;
 To live it right
 With all my might,
 Without mistake
 As for Thy sake.

"Should fear beset my way,
 May I the question lay
 Before Thy throne,
 Where all is known;
 Where what is best
 Will stand the test?

"And should the way be drear,
 Stay Thou me near.
 I hear Thy voice,
 And thus rejoice
 That I am Thine,
 And Thou art mine.

"So when my day is done,
 And to my Home I run,
 In Thee I trust
 For Thou art just;
 With me Thou art,
 And ne'er will part."

VIII

We Worship

"We took counsel together, and went into the House of the Lord in company."

THE bond of fellowship which unites Endeavorers from all parts of the continent is not the memory of shared hours of fun—hilarious moments of parade planning, fun-filled times of delegation meetings. The bond is the memory that together we worshipped God.

There are many opportunities for worship in a Christian Endeavor Convention. The morning Quiet Hour at eight o'clock is kept by the entire body of delegates. Prayer meetings, held by the State delegations, close each day. There is worship in song at each morning's general Convention session and a carefully prepared brief worship service opens each evening session. Worship is the most important part of every Convention. Worship at Grand Rapids was a vital factor in every delegate's life.

The Quiet Hour

Dr. William Hiram Foulkes presided at every Quiet Hour and himself brought the message of the first one, that of Friday morning. Mr. Homer Rodeheaver was always present to lead the singing of a few well-chosen hymns. The fact that a different speaker gave the message each morning meant that the delegates received the benefit of the counsel of several Christian leaders. The speakers were Dr. Foulkes, Dr. John R. Mulder, Dr. Norman Vincent Peale, and Dr. Frederick W. Norwood.

The Evening Worship Services

Prepared by Dr. Harry Thomas Stock, who so ably interprets youth's inarticulate aspirations, these services made blessed experiences of worship possible for the thousands of delegates and visitors who thronged the auditorium every evening.

The State Delegation Quiet Hours

"The Quiet Hour each night gave a feeling of fellowship to the delegates which seemed to be especially significant," wrote a Nebraska Intermediate, at the end of the Convention.

Other delegates shared her opinion. State after State, filling out

PART OF THE PENNSYLVANIA AND KANSAS DELEGATIONS IN THE PARADE

the brief questionnaires by which the delegates gave their opinions about the Convention, stressed the value of these "good-night" devotional meetings.

"Our devotional periods at the hotel after the evening sessions were exceedingly fine," wrote Lawrence Bash of Iowa. "We had one hundred per cent attendance. No need to urge! We had an especially significant service after the closing session of the Convention."

Dr. and Mrs. Poling and Mrs. Francis E. Clark delighted the delegates by visiting a number of the State Quiet Hour services. Dr. Norma P. Dunning and other leaders were also in attendance and by their presence added to the spiritual tone of these meetings.

IX

Forward Steps in Organization

SPLENDID as its past has been, Christian Endeavor can now look forward to even greater achievement. The plan for reorganization, put into effect at the Convention, keeps all the past values of the Christian Endeavor organization and increases its effectiveness, by the addition of a number of young people in positions of responsibility.

Dr. Daniel A. Poling was re-elected President with overwhelming enthusiasm. He has served as President of the International Society of Christian Endeavor since 1925, and of the World's Christian Endeavor Union since 1927. Under his inspired leadership Christian Endeavor has passed through one of history's most trying times without loss, indeed with substantial gains in membership and activity.

To the new office of Associate President was elected Arthur J. Stanley, twenty-six, of Dayton, Oregon. Mr. Stanley will serve for two years and will be succeeded by another leader under thirty. Mr. Stanley is a graduate of Northwestern Christian College of Eugene, Oregon, and of the University of Oregon. He has been student pastor for four years and in the fall will teach in the high school at Dayton, Oregon. He is planning to start studying for the Christian ministry in 1938.

In addition to his activity in Christian Endeavor, Mr. Stanley served as President of the National Youth Conference at Lakeside, Ohio, in 1936.

While Mr. Stanley shares the responsibilities of the Presidency of Christian Endeavor with President Poling, the Vice-Presidency will be shared by Dr. William Hiram Foulkes, Dr. A. E. Cory, and Mr. Harry N. Holmes, with nine Regional Vice-Presidents. Dr. Howard B. Grose of Providence, Rhode Island, continues as Vice-President Emeritus. The Regional Vice-Presidents are:

Region No. 1 . .	Ralph W. Arnold, Brockton, Mass.
Region No. 2 .	. Reuel B. Wolford, Wilkinsburg, Pa.
Region No. 3	. . Mrs. Frances Kreeger, Atlanta, Ga.
Region No. 4	. . Sarah E. McCullagh, Detroit, Mich.
Region No. 5 .	. . . .
Region No. 6	. . . .
Region No. 7 .	. . . .
Region No. 8 . .	Mrs. H. Spencer Clark, Scarborough, Ont., Canada
Region No. 9	Bancroft Reifsnyder, Villa Obregon, Mexico

Other officers of the International Society of Christian Endeavor are:

Associate Secretary and Superintendent of Christian Vocations, Dr. Stanley B. Vandersall.

Financial Secretary, Treasurer, and Superintendent of Travel. Carroll M. Wright.

Extension Secretary, Rev. Robert S. Nance.

EXECUTIVE COMMITTEE

Albert Arend, Spokane, Wash.
Russell J. Blair, Boston, Mass.
A. E. Cory, Indianapolis, Ind.
Bert H. Davis, Utica, N. Y.
William Hiram Foulkes, Newark, N. J.
Harry N. Holmes, New York, N. Y.
Warren G. Hoopes West Grove, Pa.
Harry W Keller, Pittsburgh, Pa.
Norman Klauder, Philadelphia, Pa.
Harry G. Kuch, Philadelphia, Pa.

Howard G. Launsbach, Brooklyn, N. Y.
Helen L. Lyon. Washington, D. C.
H. Lewis Mathewson, San Francisco, Calif.
Daniel A. Poling, Philadelphia, Pa.
Edward L. Reiner, Chicago, Ill.
Arthur J. Stanley, Dayton, Ore.
Harry Thomas Stock, Boston, Mass.
William J. von Minden, Bergenfield, N. J.
Paul M. Williams, Washington, D. C.

DEPARTMENT SUPERINTENDENTS

The following Department Superintendents are charged with the supervision of some of Christian Endeavor's most important activities:

Lookout and Extension . . . . . . Mrs. **Reba Rickman**, San Francisco, Calif.
Prayer-meeting and Devotional . . . .
Social and Recreational .   . Dr. **Darrell C. Crain**, Washington, D. C.
Missionary and Service . . . . Julia VanGenderen. Three Oaks, Mich.
Junior . . .   .
Intermediate . . . . Mrs. N. R. Gano, Clinton, N. J.
Adult-Alumni . ..   . Fred R. Roy, San Francisco, Calif.
World Peace . . . . Ernest R. Bryan, Washington, D. C.
Citizenship and Social Issues . . . . Ralph R. Gilby. Spokane, Wash.
Quiet Hour . . . . Phyllis G. Brown, Richmond, Va.
Tenth Legion .   . . . Gene Stone, Philadelphia, Pa.

More Field Secretaries

An encouraging indication of future growth for Christian Endeavor lies in the fact that today 24 States employ full-time Christian Endeavor field secretaries. To have these consecrated, self-sacrificing men and women on duty is to have the assurance of the increasing success of Christian Endeavor.

A thrilling announcement made to the Grand Rapids Convention was that of Dr. Poling, to the effect that a contribution made possible the full-time employment of Mr. Alfred T. Y. Chow as Christian Endeavor's General Secretary for China.

The contribution of $300 made by the Poling Alumni Fellowship of the Sunrise Christian Endeavor Union of Cleveland, Ohio, to Dr. Poling, will be used for extension work in one of the world's needy fields.

X

We Enjoy Good Fellowship

A DELEGATE from Massachusetts was painting signs—*and* signs—for the Oregon delegates to use on their float in the Convention parade. An Oregon delegate drew a deep, rapturous breath. "Isn't a Christian Endeavor Convention a wonderful opportunity to make friends."

Thousands of delegates would have agreed with her. Hundreds of friendships were formed between people whose homes were so far apart that they never would have met each other except for the Christian Endeavor Convention. Some romances may have begun, too, and where could romance have a better start?

Two Kansas delegates, indeed, had come to the Convention on their honeymoon. Another couple joyously admitted that they had met for the first time at the Philadelphia Convention in 1935. He (Herbert Stockton) was Convention organist; she was an out-of-town member of the Convention choir.

The Convention Parade

Everyone agreed that parade preparations were lots of fun. It was fun to march, too, even if the day had reached a new height in temperature. Kindly clouds veiled the sun soon after the march began, and enthusiastic crowds of Grand Rapids people, on reviewing stands and sidewalks and at windows overlooking the line of march, cheered the marchers.

The parade was arranged and conducted with a maximum of efficiency by Major Mallory M. Kincaid, the Grand Parade Marshal, and his associates, Major Lewis J. Donovan and Captain Ben M. Barendse. A carefully prepared booklet of "Marching Orders," including a map of the points of assembly and the line of march, made confusion impossible. Ten Division Marshals kept the divisions in perfect order. Many colorful bands of music marched, by the courtesy of co-operating organizations in Grand Rapids—the 126th Regiment of Infantry, the Salvation Army, the Sons of the American Legion, the Lions' Club, and others. A band of boys and girls in black and white uniforms and a "Kiltie" band won especial applause.

Very promptly the parade began. A squad of motorcycle police, Marshal Kincaid and his staff, parade aides, the 126th Infantry band playing the stirring hymn, "O Come, All Ye Faithful," the U. S. Naval Reserve Corps, commanded by Lieut. Commander

I. J. Van Kammen, the officers of the International Society of Christian Endeavor, Dr. Poling and Vice-Presidents, Dr. Foulkes and Mr. Holmes and their honored guests and, of particular importance, the judges of the parade.

Taking high place upon the reviewing stand beside Mrs. Poling and Mother Clark, Dr. Poling received the salute of the first delegation in line, Utah. Utah marched first because that state had made the largest number of registrations to the Convention in proportion to her quota. Red capes and white fatigue caps gave color to the delegation. The little bags of salt from Great Salt Lake which they threw to the crowds along the street gave pleasure to the watchers.

Georgia, next, with a float decorated in cotton and bearing a King and Queen of Cotton Land. Florida twirled white parasols. The state of Washington delegates rode in a car of green for the "Evergreen State."

The largest delegation from outside of Michigan appeared next. Pennsylvania, with the white-garbed girls wearing red and white "halos" and the boys red and white caps. As they passed the reviewing stand, bearing aloft signs proclaiming the activities of Christian Endeavor, Helen and Norman Klauder, Juniors, stepped up to the reviewing stand to present bouquets of lovely flowers to Mother Clark and Mrs. Poling.

Kansas, in gigantic sunflower hats; Maryland, with yellow and black capes and fatigue caps; the Golden Rule Union of Washington, D. C., magnificent in blue and gold; Tennessee and Alabama, the latter throwing stalks of cotton—a new sight to most Northerners—to the watching crowd; Nebraska in white, with black kerchiefs and caps bearing the C. E. emblem in red; two lovely girls from North Carolina; California, including Peggy Kerr, the tennis champion, in its delegation and with the beloved Paul Brown, the State Field Secretary, marching along.

Colorado, in white suits and enormous straw cowboy Stetsons; Canada, welcome delegates from the land of the maple-leaf; the District of Columbia, the girls gay in white with blue capes and red caps, the boys gayer in white trousers, blue shirts and red caps.

Kentucky of all delegations was the most charmingly costumed. Each boy was a dignified, white-clad, white-goateed "Kentucky Colonel," each girl was demure in a blue print dress, with square neckline, puffed sleeves, and long, wide skirt. Large straw bonnets framed the curls of the Kentucky belles.

North Dakota's delegates were striking in black and white Pierrot costumes. Iowa came singing its perennial chorus, "That's where the tall corn grows!" Red blouses and caps with white skirts or trousers made the delegation colorful.

Indiana, with purple capes and golden crowns; Wisconsin, in white with shaggy red chrysanthemums, released a cloud of red balloons when the seventy-six delegates reached the reviewing stand; West Virginia, with flags and parasols; Illinois, a singing delegation; Virginia, with parasols and apple blossoms; New York, very trim in white coats piped with blue; New Jersey in black and orange; Oregon, with a float showing pioneers contrasted with modern youth and a sign, "Then and Now."

Two from Texas marching proudly. Massachusetts, Missouri, Michigan.

The Michigan section made a marvelous parade all by itself, a parade especially rich in beautiful and significant floats. Port City sent a Christian Endeavor boat. Mack Evangelical Church of Detroit had a float with a cross and angels and the proclamation, "Jesus saves!" Another Detroit float showed a globe with children of all races around it. The Berrien-Cass Union's float showed the world in red and white with one attractive Miss Christian Endeavor.

From Holland came a float with a huge windmill set in a Dutch garden. Pretty Dutch children graced the garden, Dutch men and maids marched in wooden shoes around the float. Monroe County's float bore a cross with "Christ for the Crisis." From Kalamazoo, whose blue and white marching delegation threw the world-famous celery to the crowds, came a float bearing a little chapel. On Saginaw's float was a gigantic Bible. A marching delegation from Saginaw carried an enormous American flag.

Huron County, Allegan County, Central County, Bay County, from every part of the state came the Michigan delegates.

Grand Rapids proved that Christian Endeavor plays a large part in the life of the city. Several floats bore the words, "Christ for the Crisis." One, with a huge magnet, declared that Christian Endeavor is the magnet which draws young people to Christ. Emmanuel Reformed Church had a float on which appeared a picture of Calvary and the Cross, and the words, "Lest We Forget." Home Acres Reformed Church had a float bearing a model of the church.

Calvary Reformed Church's float bore a group of lovely children and the quotation, "A little child shall lead them." On another float a huge clock outlined in red flowers emphasized the idea, "Now is the Time. Christ for the Crisis." Westminster Church's float showed a model of its summer camp.

Delegates from First Presbyterian Church rode in an automobile and announced that their Christian Endeavor society is the oldest society in Michigan with a continuous life. Miss Carrie Plank, a charter member in 1881, received an ovation from the crowd.

Miss Annie Houchin from Gary, Indiana, was a guest on the

reviewing stand. Miss Houchin, who was introduced to Christian Endeavor by Dwight L. Moody, joined in October, 1881.

Doctors, lawyers, teachers, business executives and employers of Grand Rapids announced their intention to promote a Christian industrial order. Belief in the importance of Christian Education was proclaimed by a float.

Cheers greeted the Boy Scouts, pages, and ushers of the Convention. A parade of which to be proud!

Parade Awards

To delegations outside of Michigan:

For the best float, Georgia.
For the most attractive costumes, Kentucky.
For the largest delegation, Pennsylvania.

To Michigan delegations:

For the best float, Mack Avenue Evangelical Church of Detroit.
For the most attractive costumes, Holland.
For the largest delegation, Bethany Reformed Church, Grand Rapids.

Honorable mention for Grand Rapids delegation:
Westminster Presbyterian Church, Fifth Reformed Church.

The Convention Banquet

Because of the unexpected number of young people who wanted to enjoy the fellowship opportunity, the Convention Banquet actually turned into three simultaneous banquets, overflowing from the Hotel Pantlind ballroom and crowding two other large rooms.

No matter! Christian Endeavorers are proverbially good natured. In each room there were pretty girls in the smartest of gowns—the hotel was like a great flower garden that night. In each room were jolly young men ready to start a song or a cheer on the slightest provocation—or, indeed, on no provocation at all! There were honor guests in each room—International Society officers and their attractive wives. There was—if anyone noticed what he was eating—the identical menu in all three rooms. To each roomful of delegates, in turn, came Dr. and Mrs. Poling to give their greetings and to tell their story of Christian Endeavor as they had seen it on their trip around the world.

Mr. Harry N. Holmes gave a sparkling picture of Australia, the continent in which the next World's Convention of Christian Endeavor is to be held. Miss Helen L. Lyon, of Washington, D. C., who accompanied Dr. and Mrs. Poling around the world, spoke of her impressions of that trip and testified to the increasing success of Christian Endeavor everywhere.

Dr. Foulkes and Russell J. Blair gave affecting appeals for financial support of Christian Endeavor so that its activities may be increased. There was a generous response to these appeals.

It was fortunate that seats in the Convention Auditorium were reserved for the guests at the banquet, for the good time in each banquet hall was ended with reluctance. Had there been no evening session to attend, the banquet guests would have been glad to stay for hours longer!

The Pageant

When one delight ends in a Christian Endeavor Convention another almost always begins at once. So following the banquet came the pageant to which the delegates had looked forward with eager anticipation.

The Saturday evening session began like all the other evening sessions with a song period led by Mr. Homer Rodeheaver who had marched with Utah in the parade. The Convention chorus sang, beautifully as always. The Grand Rapids Convention Committee presented Mother Clark and Mrs. Poling with bouquets of red roses—armloads of exquisite red roses!

The pageant, "Christ for the Crisis," was written by Mrs. John A. Dykstra of Grand Rapids and had a cast of nearly one thousand young people. Against an artistic background two symbolic figures, youth and the Church, were placed. Youth's perplexity was well portrayed by Dean Dykstra, while the part of the Church was played with perfect dignity by Mrs. Fay Friend.

To answer Youth's questions the Church summoned four great processionals which depicted Christian Citizenship, World Peace, Church Unity, and World Fellowship.

The incidental music of the pageant was particularly appealing, as were the songs by Mr. Gordon Van Ry, baritone. The glorious finale of the pageant was the singing of the Hallelujah Chorus from "The Messiah," by the Convention choir. Each scene of the pageant had its own effectiveness; perhaps the loveliest was the last, in which hundreds of beautifully costumed young people came in a long procession representing all nations.

Special Luncheons and Dinners

Almost every mealtime was the occasion of some special fellowship festivity. An informal supper at the Y. W. C. A. on the opening night helped the delegates to get acquainted.

The pastors' luncheon was held on Friday at the Rowe Hotel. Rev. E. L. Reiner of Chicago presided, and the speakers were Dr. William Hiram Foulkes, Newark, N. J., and Dr. W. A. Mac-Taggart, Toronto, Canada.

At the same time the Junior Workers' World Fellowship luncheon took place at the Central Reformed Church. Mrs. J. C. Muste, Grand Rapids Junior Superintendent and chairman of the Junior Convention Committee, presided. "The Junior and His Wider World" was the subject of an address by Miss Ruth Seabury of Boston. A native African hymn, "We Will Praise Our Lord," was sung by Mrs. Peter Donker, Mrs. John Gilhoed, Mrs. C. Dorenbush, and Mrs. Ella Potter, all of Fifth Reformed Church.

The Intermediates' banquet on Friday evening was undoubtedly the jolliest affair of the Convention. It was held at Park Congregational Church.

Many college students attend each International Convention, and the luncheon for college students is always of unusual interest. In Grand Rapids this was held on Saturday noon at the Y. W. C. A., with Dr. J. Gordon Howard, Director of Young People's Work for the United Brethren, presiding. The principal speaker was Mr. Ernest R. Bryan, Washington, D. C., Superintendent of the Christian Endeavor World Peace Fellowship.

Another notable luncheon on Saturday was held at the Hotel Pantlind. Here gathered annual members, "Long-timers," and other guests. Mr. Paul M. Williams of Washington, D. C., presided, and the speakers included Dr. Poling, Mr. Harry W. Keller of Pittsburgh, Pa., and others.

Junior workers were entertained at tea Sunday evening by the Grand Rapids Junior Convention Committee. Following tea a service of dedication was held with Mrs. Francis E. Clark. Instrumental music by Miss Helen Keegstra, piano, Miss Anita Lamoreaux, violin, and Miss Eleanor DeBoer, 'cello, was very much enjoyed.

On Monday, another pastors' luncheon was held at the Rowe Hotel, with Mr. Harry N. Holmes and Dr. Norman Vincent Peale as the speakers.

Junior Fellowship luncheons were held on both Monday and Tuesday. On Monday the Junior workers met at Central Reformed Church, with Miss Florence VanderMolen presiding. Mrs. Inez D. Jayne, weekday and vacation school specialist of Minneapolis, spoke on "Living Together as Christian Citizens." Mr. Gerrit Raterink sang, accompanied by Miss Angeline Smits.

On Tuesday the Junior Workers lunched at Central Reformed Church, with Miss Wilma Cusser, Associate Junior Superintendent of the Michigan Christian Endeavor Union, presiding. Dr. Stanley

Committee Chairmen

Photographs through the courtesy and cooperation of the Merrild W. Coulter Studio

1. George Vruggink, *Automobile;* 2. Armen S. Kutkjian, *Badges;* 3. Clare B. Krenz, *Banquet;* 4. Rev. John H. Meengs, *Communion Service;* 5. Fred Speckin, *Decorations—Halls;* 6. Charles W. Puehl, *Exhibits;* 7. Howard C. Lawrence, *Finance;* 8. Gladys Cameron and 9. John Hendrickson, Jr., *Hotels and Housing;* 10. Marion Siekman, *Information;* 11. Richard Winters, *Intermediate;* 12. Mrs. J. C. Muste, *Junior;* 13. John R. Klaasse, *Music;* 14. Mrs. John H. Rietberg, *Pages and Guides;* 15. Mallery M. Kincaid, *Parade;* 16. Peter Verburg, *Press—Publicity;* 17. Henry W. Walstrom, *Program;* 18. Carroll Herlein, *Promotion;* 19. Rev. J. A. Dykstra, D.D., *Pulpit Supply;* 20. Stanley W. Barnett, *Radio;* 21. Herman W. Verseput, *Reception;* 22. Albert Van Dyke, *Registration—City;* 23. Mrs. C. E. Edwards, *Ushers;* 24. Angeline Smits, *Pianist.*

B. Vandersall was the guest of honor.   Music was furnished by the ladies' quartet from Fifth Reformed Church.

The Picnic at Holland

There was literally no limit to the hospitality of Grand Rapids. The Convention Committee invited the entire host of delegates to the most delightful picnic anyone could imagine.

Holland, Michigan, is a bit of the Netherlands placed, apparently by magic, actually by the efforts of early Dutch settlers and their descendants, in the very heart of the U. S. A.   Spotless streets and shining windows—quaint woolen costumes and lace caps and wooden shoes—why surely this is Vollendam or the Isle of Maarken. But no, these quaintly garbed folk are American Christian Endeavorers!

The Convention delegates loved Holland.   They bought out the town's supply of miniature windmills and Dutch dolls.   They had wooden shoes made to order and clumped around awkwardly in them—or had them covered with the autographs of other delegates and leaders.   They admired the flower gardens and enjoyed the lake.   How they demolished the sandwiches and the other delicious items in the picnic lunch!

The picnic in Holland was one of the pleasantest entertainments any Convention Committee ever devised.

GEORGIA BROUGHT THE KING AND QUEEN OF COTTON LAND

XI

What Happened in the Educational Conferences

"TO ME the conferences were the most helpful part of the Convention. In these conferences a person could ask questions and really receive the help which he wished."

The Intermediate from Nebraska who voiced this opinion could have found hundreds of like-minded delegates. The democratic procedure of the conferences made free discussion possible. You *could* ask questions—questions to be answered from the experience of other delegates or the wider experience and knowledge of the leaders. You could express your own opinions frankly and have a part in helping the group to reach the best possible conclusions regarding solution of the problems considered.

The covering theme for the entire educational plan of the Convention was the widely influential emphasis of the United Youth Movement, "Christian Youth Building a New World." The first period conferences each morning aimed to develop the general aspects and principles of the day's theme, as applicable to young people wherever found and however organized. The second period conferences were designed to seek the methods of particular application to Christian Endeavor societies and similar groups.

Each conference had a presiding chairman, a discussion leader, and a secretary—the latter a delegate who was responsible for reporting the conference to the Convention Recorder, Mrs. Catherine Miller Balm.

More than one hundred delegate secretaries made careful and complete reports. Space limitations make it impossible to present all of them in this volume, but summaries of first period conferences are given here. A number of others are quoted in Book 2 of this volume, "A Program Guide," based on discussion and action of the Grand Rapids Convention.

THEME FOR EACH DAY

Friday "Personal Christian Living."
Saturday "Building Through the Church."
Monday "A Christian Nation."
Tuesday "Christ Meeting the World's Needs."

First Period Conferences

During the first period all delegates in the Convention met in discussion groups to consider the same subject. The young people were divided alphabetically into eight conference groups, the Intermediates into six conference groups.

Friday

INTRODUCTORY STATEMENT

"Personal Christian Living"

By Dr. Harry T. Stock

As we begin our conference sessions we may ask ourselves, "Christ for *what* crisis?" Any morning paper reveals war, declared and undeclared, social confusion, dissoluteness and uncertain standards. Are we in a time like that when the prophets of Israel pronounced the doom of civilization, spoke for God and longed for justice and righteousness?

Are we in such a crisis as when Jesus called men to repent and to seek first the Kingdom of God?

In these sessions we shall be looking at certain aspects of the social obligations of our time. I hope that you will think clearly, intelligently and honestly, raising questions, sharing experiences, discovering the answer to "What does Christianity mean for me, my church and the world?"

Today we consider personal religion. Here are three possible questions whose answers you might seek:

1. What difference must Christianity make in my own life?

Christians must be different. Jesus called them "leaven" and "salt." First century Christians *were* different. Will there be observable differences in us while we are in Grand Rapids? Are there non-Christians anywhere who live more justly and unselfishly than we do?

2. How do we grow in Christian character and strength?

3. How are we going to share our religion?

EXTRACTS FROM THE REPORTS ON

"Personal Christian Living"

There are two types of religious experience which influence our thought and action: (1) The Way of Negation, by which we mean that religion's chief contribution to life is to impose taboos, to say, "Don't do this!" (2) The Way of Affirmation, by which we mean those positive personal experiences of faith by which we live and in which we find our joy.

Some of the affirmative things we do are (a) Pray, (b) Study the Bible, (c) Practice the Golden Rule, (d) Practice our concepts of moral integrity—honesty, etc., (e) Attend church, (f) Forget self and give ourselves to others, (g) Live out Christlikeness.

The outward appearances by which we are recognized as Christians include (a) The company we keep, (b) Our type of recreation, (c) Our habits and language. We may grow in the Christian life by (a) Associating with other Christians and studying our fellow-men, (b) Exercising the powers we have—using our talents, praying in public, leading young people's meetings, doing something for others, not from a sense of duty but from love keeping the Quiet Hour, sharing with others our knowledge of Jesus.

It is not easy to be a Christian. Some of the difficulties are criticism, being shunned by people whose good opinion we desire, the problems of conflicting ideals and split loyalties, the common un-Christian practices of modern business. To be a Christian requires discipline, self-sacrifice. But it is well for us to remember that when we face the crisis in our individual life we are not facing it alone. Jesus is with us.

The purpose of Christian Endeavor to build a new world is fulfilled as we build new individuals.

What difference ought "being a Christian" to make?

It should give us a sense of divine kinship and destiny, and enable us to realize our personal worth to God. We should have a conscious personal relationship with Him. Being aware of this relationship we should do nothing to destroy it, and everything in our power to fulfill it. We should have faith in the ultimate triumph of righteousness and goodness.

We should be conscious of our social responsibility. Our relationship to God challenges us to a finer relationship with our fellow-men. The Fatherhood of God is the basis for the brotherhood of men. Our inward convictions should be expressed in love and service and sacrifice.

We are handicapped in achieving complete Christian living by selfish interests, sinful indulgence, a lack of the sense of the reality of God, seemingly unanswered prayer, the example of professed but insincere Christians, and the apparent success of non-Christians. The problem of the suffering of good people bewilders us, and we have difficulty in deciding what is right and what is wrong in the face of today's confused moral codes. We sometimes fail to realize the necessity of *cultivating* the Christian life and our worship becomes meaningless.

Jesus Christ is the supreme demonstration of personal Christian living. He lived a normal life, with a definitely social outlook, making contacts with all kinds of people and particularly enjoying the home-life of his friends. Emotionally He was stable and well-poised. He never fought for His own personal defense but was vigorous in defense of the rights of others. He was indignant at all false and wrong practices but had infinite sympathy for the sick, the poor, the sinful,— a heart of love for all men. His spiritual life was nourished by regular church attendance, and by a deep prayer-life. He went about doing good, serving not only His friends but also His enemies.

What can we do to grow in Christian life? We can be obedient to the will of God, consciously seeking through prayer and scripture and meditation to learn what His will for us is. Our prayer must be dialogue, we must listen as well as ask, we must constantly practice prayer and meditation. We must be sincerely in earnest in seeking to grow. Our love must spend itself in friendly living and loving service. Giving expression to the Christian life in word and deed will strengthen and crystallize our own convictions. Our fellowship in the church will encourage us to grow. Finally, we must have the spirit of sacrifice. We must be willing to suffer for the sake of helping to bring about God's will and the Kingdom of God.

SOME SUGGESTED RESOURCES

The Bible, including the newer translations.

"A Guide to Youth Action in Personal Religious Living," pamphlet in the "Christian Youth Building a New World" series.

"I Am a Christian," Wilson.

"The Challenge and Power of Jesus," Gilkey.

Saturday

INTRODUCTORY STATEMENT

"Building Through the Church"

By Dr. Harry T. Stock

The church was born in a crisis; it exists to meet crises; it is itself in a crisis! Today we are to look at some of the responsibilities of young people toward the church of today and tomorrow. How can youth help the church to meet the crisis of personal life and social need?

The church is being criticized. It is said that the church has lost its hold upon the people, that its influence is lessened. The American Youth Commission reports, "The churches and schools are no longer furnishing adequate aid in developing character."

There is some justification for criticism of the church but the critics fail to see some facts. People still die. The church is the only agency to help people to be in fellowship with God and each other. All the best we have comes to us through the church. The leaders of the church have been prophets; all social action comes through church leadership.

In our discussion groups we should look frankly at the church. Let us consider:

1. What can young people do to make the church adequate for the crisis of personal and social life?
2. Will the Protestant church endure?
3. What are young people to do about the church?
4. What is the position of the church in the modern world?
5. What are young people to do with reference to a more united church?

EXTRACTS FROM REPORTS ON
"Building Through the Church"

What kind of "building" is needed? A higher type of personal living, the raising of the level of life in the community, the curing of social ills,—the sins of man against man, such as jealousy, envy, greed, race discrimination, the hatred that leads to war.

The church is the one enduring agency; it must apply itself to questions of both the present and eternity. It is the one authoritative agency and deserves our first loyalty. However, there must be improvement in its organization and program.

There must be a place for young people and a leadership capable of training young people to occupy their place.

The church must daringly combat present-day sins.

One way to get people to come to church is to show the people by your example that you have something that they need.

Usually the church at its worst is better than the community at its best.

The church must speak with assured authority on the larger questions of human relationships as in industry, agriculture, class prejudices, sectional differences national problems and international relationships. A silent religion gets nowhere.

The Christian church in its local activities, in its interchurch and interdenominational activities may well become a training place where individual Christians and groups of Christians get first-hand experience in the techniques of a Christian social order. A local church that is vitally concerned that the affairs of its own community be Christian is growing members about whom we need have no fear as to their ultimate concern about the wider affairs of the state, nation and the world.

The Christian church must train and send out Christian statesmen as well as Christian missionaries.

Young people can help to build up the church by (1) Serving as friendly helpers to younger people in the church, (2) Personal religious living, (3) Supporting the church in all its activities, (4) Assuming leadership responsibilities, (5) Co-operating with the adults.

SOME SUGGESTED RESOURCES

"Builders of a New World," Bartlett.

"Group Action in Building a New World," pamphlet in the "Christian Youth Building a New World" series.

"Christianity in Our World," Bennett.

"What Must the Church Do to Be Saved?" Tittle.

Monday

EXTRACTS FROM REPORTS ON

"A Christian Nation"

Church membership does not necessarily make a nation Christian. Some of the characteristics of a Christian nation are: People living as followers of Christ, leaders who follow Christian principles, high ideals and good laws. A Christian nation is composed of people committed to the will of God.

Do we have a Christian Nation? What about these? (1) The liquor traffic, (2) Unchristian leadership in politics, (3) Strikes and other evidences of strife between capital and labor, (4) Increasing crime, (5) Race prejudice and discrimination, (6) The Oriental Exclusion Act, (7) Child labor, (8) Divorce, (9) Increasing armaments. Are these the characteristics of a Christian nation?

The Christian way to get rid of Communism is not to try to destroy the Communist but to crush the evils of injustice and prejudice out of which Communism grows.

SOME SUGGESTED RESOURCES

"Youth Action in Breaking Down Barriers."*
"Youth Action on the Use of Leisure Time."*
"Youth Action on the Liquor Problem."*
Publications of Allied Youth, Inc., National Education Association Building, Washington, D. C.
"A Christian's Patriotism," E. L. Shaver.

Tuesday

EXTRACTS FROM REPORTS ON

"Christ Meeting the World's Needs"

We must get acquainted with our neighbors here; our relationship with them is symbolic of the relations between nations. Then we must overcome our prejudices against other nations.

Each nation is "peculiar"—to the other nations. The great enterprise of foreign missions is one way of helping nations to know each other   The support of foreign missions—eighty-nine per cent of the money and most of the trained leaders must come from the church here—is our opportunity to help.

Missionary education can be increased in our home churches by the study of books on missions, regular meetings with missionary topics, a school of missions in the local church or community, pageants and plays, the visits of missionaries on furlough. Interesting information can be secured by sending kodaks and rolls of film to missionaries so that they can send back pictures of their work. We can practice missionary work in our own community.

There are some definite things we can do for peace in our own societies: (a) Educate the society itself. You can't do that in one meeting on a peace topic! It means thorough study. (b) Discourage the use of military togs. One society rented a store with a glass front in a prominent place in town. At Christmas they displayed military togs, surrounding them with posters showing the horrors of war. Other posters emphasized the Christian attitude toward war. (c) Give prominence to the heroes of peace. (d) Try to influence public opinion. Have a reading table with books on peace for the members of the church; give peace plays; place peace literature in public places; promote the right kind of home education. (e) Have a Peace Fellowship in your society.

*Pamphlets in the "Christian Youth Building a New World" series.

We are no longer isolated communities, so we must give up our small loyalties for larger loyalties. The economic problems of the world can be solved only by united effort. We must build a World Fellowship.

Second Period Conferences
Friday
"Better Devotional Meetings"

Because of the great need in young people's groups for help in realizing the possibilities of the devotional meeting, or prayer meeting, and in knowing how to plan and conduct these meetings, all the conferences of the second period on Friday except two special ones, "The Fellowship of Prayer," and the "Pastors' Conference," were given over to a thorough study of this subject. Divided alphabetically, the delegates met in twelve conferences in the Young People's Division and six conferences in the Intermediate Division.

EXTRACTS FROM REPORTS ON
"Better Devotional Meetings"

Some of the desired objectives of society devotional meetings are: (a) Deepening the spiritual life of the individual, (b) Helping individual growth through leadership training, (c) Developing powers of expression, (d) Seeking out courses of action, (e) Gaining the interest of others, (f) Securing the values of Christian fellowship and comradeship, (g) Participating in experiences and sharing the values of worship, (h) Establishing examples of Christian living, (i) Training for Endeavor leadership, (j) Learning the history and present program of the church, (k) Sharing in the missionary enterprise, (l) Facing up to current life in all its aspects and seeking the Christian interpretation of and solution for problems.

In selecting topics keep in mind the objectives listed. Be sure that the scope of the topics for the year is sufficiently comprehensive. The Christian Endeavor Topics have a wide scope; they are carefully selected and there are ample materials available to help in preparing to discuss them. However you may substitute other topics as local need requires. A check list is useful in discovering the interests and needs of your members. In selecting topics keep in mind your local church program, the seasons, etc.

Use a variety of helps in preparing for discussion, such as *The Christian Endeavor World*, denominational and interdenominational papers, current magazines, experiences of life.

Select leaders on the basis of interest, competency, need. Do not over-urge. Some members have to be guided slowly through lesser phases of leadership before leading a meeting.

Have a research committee to collect facts for topic-discussions and pass them on to the leaders.

Take a few minutes at the close of each meeting to announce the next topic. Suggest lines of thought or questions.

A worship meeting should generate activity and lead us out to highways of service and usefulness.

The devotional meeting is the heart of the Christian Endeavor society.

Saturday and Monday

General Theme: "Successful Christian Endeavor"

Many different subjects dealing with methods of Christian Endeavor work were offered in the second period conferences on Saturday and Monday. Most of the conferences were continued on the same subject through both periods. Conference subjects, leaders and chairmen were as follows:

YOUNG PEOPLE'S DIVISION

Leading Society Meetings

Leader: Warren G. Hoopes, Field Secretary. Pennsylvania Union.
Chairman: Miss Mary D. Brown, Utah.

Training Society Officers

Leader: Frederick L. Mintel, Executive Secretary, New Jersey Union.
Chairman: John E. Abnett, Kentucky.

Using Leisure Time Well

Leader: Dr. Norman E. Richardson, Professor of Christian Education, Presbyterian Theological Seminary. Chicago.
Chairman: (Saturday) Albert Arend, Washington; (Monday) Rev. W. N. Tice, Kansas.

How to Organize a Society

Leader: Rev. Lawrence Bash, Field Secretary, Iowa Union.
Chairman: Howard Cole, Oregon.

Recruiting and Training Members

Leader: Rev. Vernon L. Phillips, Field Secretary, Connecticut Union.
Chairman: Miss Sibyl Smith, Nebraska.

Christian Endeavor in the Total Program of the Church

Leader: Rev. Myron T. Hopper, Director Young People's Work. Disciples of Christ.
Chairman: J. W. Eichelberger, Jr.

Informing the Public

Leader: Rev. Willard E. Rice, Associate Minister, Marble Collegiate (Reformed) Church, New York City.
Chairman: Harvey W. Marks, Colorado.

Best Methods of Missionary Activity

Leader: Dr. Norma P. Dunning, Mary Wanless Hospital, India.
Chairman: Miss Sarah McCullagh, Michigan.

Helping Others to Choose Christ

Leader: Rev. Andrew J. Kurth, Minister, Twelfth Street Evangelical Church, Detroit, Mich.
Chairman: Miss Margaret Reynolds, Missouri.

Vocations in the New Day

Leader: Rev. Franklin J. Hinkamp, Minister, Niskayuna Reformed Church Schenectady, N. Y.
Chairman: Mr. Guy Leavitt, Editor, *The Outlook.*

Union Work in Christian Endeavor

Leader: Ernest S. Marks, Executive Secretary, Michigan Union.
Chairman: Howard Launsbach, New York.

Methods of Alcohol Education

Leader: W. Roy Breg, Executive Secretary, Allied Youth, Inc.
Chairman: Martin Harvey.

Working for Peace

Leaders: (Saturday) Dr. Frank D. Getty, Director of Young People's Work, Presbyterian Church, U. S. A. (Monday) Dr. Raymond M. Veh, Editor, *The Evangelical Crusader.*
Chairman: Herbert L. Minard, Editor, *The Front Rank.*

Looking Toward Marriage

Leader: Rev. Clifford Earle, Minister, First Congregational Church, Racine, Wisconsin.
Chairman: George R. Sweet, Indiana.

Meeting Local Problems in Citizenship

Leader: Rev. E. L. Reiner, Minister, Waveland Avenue Congregational Church, Chicago, Ill.
Chairman: Harold F. Jackson, Georgia.

A Complete Society Program

Leader: Dr. Albert J. Anthony, Minister, First Presbyterian Church, Alma, Mich.
Chairman: Harry G. Kuch Pennsylvania.

The Devotional Life of the Individual

Leader: Dr. John R. Mulder, Professor of Practical Theology, Western Theological Seminary, Holland, Mich.
Chairman: Miss Marguerite Keeney, Iowa.

Practical Methods of Stewardship

Leader: Dr. E. E. Harris, Editor, *The Watchword.*
Chairman: Miss Elizabeth Cooper, .Nebraska.

INTERMEDIATE DIVISION

A Complete Society Program

Leader: Rev. Earle W. Gates, Executive Secretary, New York State Union.
Chairman: Dr. S. S. Morris.

Training Christian Endeavor Officers

Leader: Rev. Robert S. Nance, Extension Secretary, International Society.
Chairman: George Wilson, Dixie.

Using Leisure Time Well

Leader: Mrs. Franklin J. Hinkamp, Schenectady, N. Y.
Chairman: Harold S. Day, Wisconsin

Recruiting and Training Members

Leaders: (Saturday) Dr. J. Gordon Howard, Director of Young People's Work, United Brethren Church; (Monday) Russell J. Blair, Field Secretary, Massachusetts Union.

Chairmen: (Saturday) Lewis Mathewson, California; (Monday) James A. Brown, D. C.

Informing the Public

Leader: Dr. Paul C. Brown, Field Secretary, California Union.
Chairman: Mrs. Dorothy MacKenzie, New Hampshire.

Missionary Methods for Intermediates

Leader: Miss Ruth I. Seabury, Educational Secretary, American Board of Commissioners for Foreign Missions.
Chairman: Reuel B. Wolford, Pennsylvania.

Helping Others to Choose Christ

Leaders: (Saturday) Rev. Chester Rutledge, Field Secretary, Washington Union; (Monday) Rev. Aldis L. Webb, Field Secretary, Texas Union.
Chairman: Miss Mary Rogillio, Louisiana.

"A Windmill in a Garden, Crailed by Dutch Children"
The Holland Delegation in the Parade

Problems in Personal Conduct

Leader: Rev. Ivan M. Gould, Associate Director of Young People's Work, International Council of Religious Education.

Chairman: Rev. Harley Sutton.

The Devotional Life of the Intermediate

Leader: Rev. Hugh B. Kilgour, Minister, Central Church of Christ, Grand Rapids, Mich.

Chairman: T. Shepherd Clark, Georgia.

Excerpts from a number of these conferences, directly affecting objectives in the new program of Christian Endeavor, are quoted in the second book of this report ("A Program Guide").

"Our Hopes Have Become History"
DOCTOR STANLEY B. VANDERSALL, MR. CARROLL M. WRIGHT, AND DOCTOR DANIEL A. POLING
APPROVING THE CONVENTION PROGRAM

XII

Junior Features in the Convention

The Junior Session

THE Junior features of the Grand Rapids Convention began with the Juniors themselves when they gathered for luncheon in the Central Reformed Church, and then marched, with motorcycle escort, to the Civic Auditorium for their own session under the direction of Mrs. J. C. Muste, Junior Chairman of the Convention Committee, and Miss Florence Vander Molen, Junior Superintendent for Michigan.

The programs for the session had been bound in covers bearing Hofmann's Boy Christ in color, so that each Junior could frame the picture for his own Prayer Corner at home.

The seven hundred Juniors drew Dr. Poling from the Trustees' Meeting for a warm and friendly greeting, and listened with appreciation to "Mother" Clark's message on "Whatever He Would Like To Have Me Do." She told the story of Alice Freeman Palmer's Three Recipes for Happiness: Do something for someone every day; look for something beautiful every day; learn something to remember every day. She hoped that every Endeavorer would find happiness through serving Christ and in doing whatever He would like to have him do.

A Junior Choir of fifty voices, assembled from the various Grand Rapids Junior societies and trained by Mr. J. C. Muste, sang the "Hymn for the Nations" and blended the colors of the national flags as they sang. By request this number was repeated on Monday evening in the main Convention.

The Moslem play, "Tara Finds the Door to Happiness," was a beautiful and effective illustration of the Junior theme, "Sharing Christ," which hung above the platform. The Junior Christian Endeavor societies of Central Reformed and East Congregational churches had made the most interesting scenery and attractive costumes, and presented the play, all under the direction of Miss Eunice Brockmier and Mrs. G. Janssen. Shirley DeVries of Calvary Reformed Church gave added expression to the theme in the "Pledge to All Lands."

Quiet piano and violin music by Miss Eleanor DeBoer and Miss Anita Lamoreaux carried the reverent mood of the play over into the Worship Service, when the Juniors made their personal commitment to the purpose of sharing Christ. The boys and girls were very responsive to the leadership of Mrs. Inez D. Jayne, in Scripture, where Christ was portrayed as He shared Himself—

103

healing, teaching, preaching, as our Saviour, and as He gave the Commission to His followers, that they too might share; in hymn, and in prayer. In the meditation, Mrs. Jayne spoke of Eugene Burnand's great painting, "Go Preach," in which the young man is shown the world of today and is told: "You will have not only to speak with your lips but teach with your life," and said to the Juniors, "This, Juniors also can do!"

The Round Tables for State Superintendents

Nineteen States, Ontario and Panama, were represented in the first morning hours, when subjects such as the following were elected and discussed freely and with intense interest:

How to arouse the interest of today's young people in Junior Work,

What sort of State Program affords the best guidance and stimulation to the societies?

New materials most needed in the Junior field,

How can State organizations function most effectively?

What relationship should there be between the Junior society activities and meetings?

By what criteria should we judge and choose Topic materials?

The fellowship of this group is one of the most stimulating experiences of an International Convention. Recognition of the State Junior leaders was made by the International Society in a dinner on Friday evening, when they sat down with Mrs. Clark, Dr. and Mrs. Poling, and Dr. and Mrs. Vandersall.

Conferences for Junior Workers

The Junior Service Room in the Civic Auditorium was comfortably furnished to meet the several requirements of the Junior program, and the advantage taken of its services kept the hostesses, Mrs. T. London, Mrs. J. Janssen, Mrs. J. Slott, and both Junior Committee and Junior Staff in constant attendance.

The Program of Objectives for Christian Endeavor Societies and Unions, 1937–1939, as approved by the Board of Trustees, was presented by Dr. Stanley B. Vandersall, Associate Secretary of the International Society of Christian Endeavor. (This is described in Book 2 of this report, "A Program Guide.")

The Theme for the Biennium is "Christ for the Crisis." Defining this theme for Juniors, it means Christ for all our needs. Since Juniors learn that which they do, this meaning is translated into action, and becomes "We Share Christ." (See Christian Endeavor's Program for Juniors, page 109.)

To help in making the theme effective during the next two years in the areas of personal religious living, church loyalty, service to our country, and sharing with the world, a unit on "Sharing Christ" was prepared for use in Junior Christian Endeavor Devotional Meetings, and as a resource to be drawn upon for the programs and activities of both Societies and Unions.

The author of the unit, Mrs. Inez D. Jayne, used forty Grand Rapids Juniors, who had been assembled by Miss Eleanor DeBoer, to demonstrate Session II, "We Learn to Know Him in the Church," illustrating various methods and techniques. Mrs. Jayne, Week Day and Vacation Church School specialist, was the Conference leader and gave invaluable help, both in the preparation of the Junior program and throughout the Convention days.

The adults were divided into two groups to make effective demonstration possible. Even so, the rooms were crowded to capacity, and the interest was very evident in the discussion of the methods and materials used in the Demonstration Hours.

In response to the expressed need, an Activity Schedule was suggested for the year, September, 1937, through August, 1938. (See page 110.)

On the Demonstration mornings, the second group considered the sources and use of materials with Juniors. The "sharing" in this group was most helpful. Mrs. Janssen brought the scenery, made by her Juniors for Thursday's play, to show that it was simple enough for any group anywhere to make and use. Mrs. Martin of Illinois had brought a wealth of material, and the exhibits and literature were handled with the keenest of interest.

Fellowship Luncheons

Miss Marion Siekman and her sub-committee and Mrs. William V. Martin of illinois collaborated to provide a party atmosphere for the three luncheons, and the ladies of Central Reformed Church served delicious meals. Friday found us "in Holland," with a Dutch windmill turning its vanes, wooden shoes filled with gay tulips, blue and white Dutch caps for everyone and Dutch boy and girl dolls as surprise favors. Mrs. J. C. Muste presided as the hostess and presented her Junior Committee. The introductions were acknowledged and appreciation was expressed to Mrs. Muste and her Committee on behalf of the International Society, the Junior Staff and the luncheon guests. The ladies' quartet from Fifth Reformed Church, Mrs. Peter Donker, Mrs. John Gilhoed, Mrs. C. Dorenbush, Mrs. Ella Potter, and Mrs. B. Van Oss, accompanist, sang a native African hymn from manuscript, and responded to the encore with a Dutch song.

The guest speaker was Miss Ruth Isabel Seabury, Boston, Massachusetts, Educational Secretary of the American Board, who spoke of "The Junior and His Wider World." Missionary education of boys and girls should be characterized by three attitudes, a realization that America does not possess Christianity, a sympathetic understanding and appreciation of other peoples, and a lack of any sense of superiority, according to Miss Seabury. She quoted the Chinese college girl at conference who flung these searching questions at her: "Do they still lynch in America?" "Is the church in America still divided?" "Did you ever see a successful love marriage?" and cited other challenging experiences in India. Special attention was called to the Missionary Education books for children, with mention of the Rainbow Series, the Nursery Series, "Missionary Stories to Tell," and recommendation to the leaders of "Heritage of Beauty" by Daniel Johnson Fleming.

In a patriotic setting on Monday, Miss Florence Vander Molen, Michigan State Junior Superintendent, introduced Mrs. Jayne as the guest speaker, with the subject, "Living Together as Christian Citizens." In brief the substance of her message was as follows: Everyday problems of boys and girls in the areas of family, school, church, community, national and world living are much more difficult than confronted earlier generations. Awareness through the radio, press, "funnies," and movies is inevitable. Leaders must help them examine the world and face problems; discuss certain issues critically; meet differing social situations without emotional strain; and improve their own circumstances. This study should be a sincere inquiry—not with the idea of asserting one's own opinion—but to understand the great principles which dominated Jesus, and to determine what one as a Christian should think and do about particular situations. There is high adventure for Juniors in the study of community and world problems—social, economic, and relating to peace,—particularly as they affect children.

The solos of Mr. Gerrit Raterink of Bethany Reformed Church, accompanied by Miss Angeline Smits, were greatly enjoyed.

Tuesday's luncheon with its nautical motif was planned especially for Union Junior Superintendents. Miss Wilma Cusser, Associate Junior Superintendent for Michigan, presided as hostess, and Dr. and Mrs. Stanley B. Vandersall were the honored guests. Following the luncheon, the Union Superintendents spent an hour in conference, addressing their attention particularly to a questionnaire about the Junior features of Conventions—looking toward a co-operative bulletin on this subject. The Revised Union Junior Superintendents' Bulletin was distributed at this time.

The Parents' Hour
(Sunday Afternoon)

The parents were received by the hostess, Mrs. D. Blocksma of the Grand Rapids Committee, and were seated by the State Junior Superintendents under the direction of Miss Vander Molen, as they assembled for their hour in the Black and Silver Room of the Civic Auditorium. The music was furnished by Miss Eleanor DeBoer of Grand Rapids, pianist; Mr. John Weaver of Lansing, violinist; Mrs. Harold E. Veldman, of Bethel Reformed Church, soloist; and Dr. Harold E. Veldman, accompanist.

Dr. Daniel A. Poling, President of the World's Christian Endeavor Union, presided and presented the speakers, Mrs. Inez D. Jayne, Minneapolis, Minnesota, and Dr. Albert J. Anthony, Alma, Michigan, Pastor, First Presbyterian Church, who addressed an appreciative audience of five hundred on the following subjects:

"The Kingdom of God in Our Homes"—Mrs. Jayne (brief summary).

The inherent right of every child to training to enable him to stand firm under the pressures of life—the greatest of which are fear of popular disapproval and failure,—must cause parents to seek a cure for these fears. The rating of a good home is determined by the degree of security which the child feels there.

No parents seeking highest good can find better help than a worthy religion. Christianity provides sense of dependability of the universe, makes one conscious of companionship with God, invites and interprets experiences so that one becomes a co-operator with God in His great purposes, offers Jesus as Friend, Guide, Teacher, and Saviour.

"Oh, that the picture of Christ
Were painted clearly on the wall
Of every living room on earth,
Where one could never fail at all
To see Him there—His gentle eyes
Following one throughout the days;
Surely those eyes would influence
A family's manners, words, and ways.

"Oh, that all parents of the earth
Would feed their young the Bread of
Life;

Give Living Water for their thirst.
If every husband, every wife
Were so Christ-filled that they could
live
His life for all the world to see;
If they would give their children,
Christ,
How transformed would the old
world be!"

GRACE NOLL CROWELL
(From *Christian Herald*)

Parents fall into three classes, parents of caprice, who do not take Him into account, parents with a noble attitude toward life, but unrelated to His purpose or plan, and parents who are conscious of His love and care and co-operate in each experience as sons of God, eager to help in the establishment of His Kingdom on the earth.

Christianity is not a set of ideas changing with the times, but a set of ideals toward which parents and children must consciously strive, that the home may become a part of the Kingdom, offering to the child the greatest sense of security, the fullest sense of co-operation with God, the most abundant life.

"A Little Prayer-Nook in the Home"—Dr. Anthony.   (In abbreviated outline.)

"Train up a child in the way he should go: and when he is old, he will not depart from it.

Importance of Early Religious Training:

What we learn in childhood gives the only ultimate satisfactions in later life.   Paul to Timothy—I Tim. 4:7; II Tim. 1:5.

Train up the child in the home so that he knows "This is my Father's world," and so that his devotional habits are so much a part of his everyday experiences that he never knows himself to be anything other than a Christian.

Contribution of Junior Christian Endeavor to This Goal:

Most of us learned to enjoy prayer and other devotional elements in Junior Christian Endeavor, as a group experience.

Junior worship experience is real, vital and satisfying.

Necessity to Go Beyond the Group Experience into Personal Fellowship:

Many adults do not practice personal devotions; never learned how.

Parents may train Juniors in private devotions in the home, and perhaps learn for themselves, if they remember one of the laws of learning, the law of association.

A little Prayer-Nook may be set up in the home, the child's own little sanctuary.

It may be a corner of his bedroom, or even under the stairs.

There may be an orange box altar, a Bible, a picture, drape, or Cross.

Daily readings, brief prayers, prayer suggestions, devotional reading material, may be placed there.

It is important that the child be allowed to use the Prayer-Nook without persuasion or notice by the family, so that the practice becomes a normal part of the home life.

A little Prayer-Nook in the home can raise humble little lives into lives of power.

The Vesper Service of Dedication

The Junior Workers were invited to be the guests of the Grand Rapids Junior Committee at tea on Sunday evening. Miss Keegstra at the piano, Miss DeBoer on the cello, and Mr. Weaver on the violin, played a program of sacred music during the tea and in the Vesper Service.

This hour was a restful, friendly time of Christian fellowship. The Service used had been sent to all State Superintendents that they might keep the Hour with us, wherever they were. "Mother" Clark gave an intimate, personal message, which no Junior Worker will forget, and used Paul's words as her charge:

"Only let your manner of life be worthy of the gospel of Christ: that ye stand fast in one spirit, with one mind striving together for the faith of the gospel;

"And this I pray, that your love may abound yet more and more in knowledge and in all judgment;

"That ye may approve things that are excellent; that ye may be sincere and without offence till the day of Christ;

"Being filled with the fruits of righteousness, which are by Jesus Christ, unto the glory and praise of God."

Grateful acknowledgment is made to the Officers of the International Society of Christian Endeavor, the members of the Junior Staff, and the very considerable number of individuals and agencies whose generous and helpful co-operation made possible the success of this Junior program.

"Christft for the Crisis"

CHRISTIAN ENDEAVOR'S PROGRAM OBJECTIVES, 1937–1939
ADAPTED TO THE USE OF JUNIORS AND JUNIOR SOCIETIES

"Whatever He would like to have me do"

The theme for the biennium is applied in four areas:

Personal religious living, including definite commitment to Christ;
Loyalty to the church and its work;
Practical Christian service which reaches our fellowmen and loyally supports our country;
World-wide sharing of the Christian spirit and program.

When defining the theme for Juniors, it means Christ for all our needs. Since Juniors learn that which they do, we need to translate this meaning into action.

Thus " *We Share Christ*" is suggested as the theme for the Juniors.

When applied to the four areas in which it operates, the activity becomes progressive:

We accept Christ as our personal Saviour.
We learn to know Him in the church.
We serve Him loyally in our country.
We share Him with the world.

Help to vitalize this theme and to make it effective in each Junior society is provided in a four-session unit, "Sharing Christ," which may be used as a whole or in part in Junior society devotional meetings, and as a resource for the programs and activities of societies and unions.

In response to a need repeatedly expressed by state and union superintendents, an activity schedule is suggested for the year, September, 1937, through August, 1938. An effort has been made to harmonize the topics and monthly emphases. This suggested activity is to be adapted to suit the needs of the individual states.

Suggested Junior Activity Schedule

SEPTEMBER, 1937

SURVEY AND REORGANIZATION (We learn to know Him in the church).

  a. Make survey map of church district; list prospective members and strive to win them. (This map may be made to serve the entire church.)
  b. Provide public graduation for Juniors ready for promotion. (An Order of Service appears in *The Junior Worker's Notebook*, pp. 30, 31.)
  c. Adapt suggested goals to need of church and society; assign duties.
    (See *To Build the Program for Your Junior Society*.)
  d. Introduce the monthly *Christian Endeavor World* to every superintendent.

NOTE: *Junior Societies of Christian Endeavor.*
Unit, *Learning Together about Jesus, Our Friend.*
Installation Service for Officers of Junior Societies of Christian Endeavor.

Junior Christian Endeavor Topics:
    5. Renewing Our Endeavors. Phil. 3 : 13-15 (Consecration Meeting).
    12. How Can We Reach Others? John 1 : 35-42.
    19. Growing as Jesus Grew. Luke 2 : 52.
    26. Choosing Our Goals. Phil. 4 : 8.

OCTOBER

TRAINING IN WORLD FRIENDSHIP (We share Him with the world).
  a. Make systematic and definite plans for providing information, guiding activities and developing right attitudes.
  b. Begin Mission Study: *We Sing America.*
                    A Junior Teacher's Guide on Negro Americans.

(See Missionary Education Announcement of Books, Maps. Plays, Pictures, and other Teaching Material for 1936–1937.)

c. Plan adequate and helpful program of recreation.

d. Co-operate in the choice of materials to be memorized (particularly with the Junior department of the Sunday Church School).

Each society should consult its own Denominational Board for literature and helps in their Mission Study program. File carefully all materials and save for future reference.

Junior Christian Endeavor Topics:

3. How Negroes in America Have Climbed Upward. Ps. 40 : 1–3. (Consecration Meeting.)

10. Negroes at Work and at Play. Prov. 3 : 1–7.

17. Negro Songs and Poetry. Ps. 96 : 1–9.

24. Goodwill toward the Negro. Luke 2 : 14.

31. Negroes as Fellow-Americans. Luke 10 : 30–37.

NOVEMBER

TRAINING IN THE RIGHT USE OF GOD'S GIFTS (We share Him with the world).

a. Develop the desire to be "workers together with God": enroll Juniors as members of the Tenth Legion.

b. Make weekly offering climax for the worship service.

c. Help the Juniors draw up society budget.

d. Cultivate regular systematic giving by using the pledge-envelope system.

NOTE: *Riches to Share*. Alice B. Hobensack (Abingdon Press).
A Guide for Teachers; Pupil's Work Book.

Junior Christian Endeavor Topics:

7. Victories of Peace. 1 John 4 : 7, 8, 20, 21. (Consecration Meeting.)
   (Suggest *Victories of Peace*, Gill and Pullen.)

14. God's Gift of Life. Acts 17 : 24–29.

21. God's Gifts of Time and Talent. Matt. 25 : 14–30.

28. God's Gift of Money. Luke 12 : 16–21.

NOTE: *An Egyptian Thanksgiving*. Elsie M. Bush.
The Hebrew Feast of the Ingathering. Jessie Dell Crawford.
Our American Thanksgiving. Charlotte C. Jones, included in *The Thanksgiving Festival as an Introduction to Comparative Religions* from the Congregational Publishing Society.

DECEMBER

TRAINING IN SERVICE FOR OTHERS (We share Him with the world).
   a. Plan for missionary gifts of money, material, service and sunshine through denominational boards (see denominational literature).
   b. Participate in "World Friendship Among Children" Projects. (See announcement folder, *Sending Gifts to Spanish Refugee Children*, from Committee on World Friendship Among Children, 297 Fourth Avenue, New York City.)
   c. Educate for Peace.
      (See Missionary Education Announcement, 1937–1938.)

NOTE: *Learning about War and Peace*. Imogene M. McPherson (Bethany Press).
Changing Swords into Plowshares, four units (Pilgrim Press).
NOTE the classified list of Service Activities for Juniors in the *Christian Endeavor World Quarterly*—issues of the last two quarters in 1935, and the third quarter in 1936. Please keep a memorandum of other activities engaged in, and report them.

Junior Christian Endeavor Topics:
   5. Using God's Gifts for Him. Matt. 25 : 31–45. (Consecration Meeting.)
   12. Why Did God Give His Son to the World? John 3 : 14–17.
   19. Making This Christmas a Happy One. Luke 2 : 8–20.
   26. Have I Done My Best in 1937? John 15 : 5; Phil. 4 : 13.

NOTE: *Christmas with Juniors*. (Board of Education, Methodist Episcopal Church).
December Services of Worship for Junior Boys and Girls, (same source).
The Road to Bethlehem, (Bethany Press).

JANUARY, 1938

TRAINING IN WORSHIP (We accept Christ as our personal Saviour).
   a. Train Juniors to participate with understanding in, and to conduct, services of worship.

NOTE: *Worship Training for Juniors*. Josephine L. Baldwin.
Guiding the Experience of Worship, Marie Cole Powell.

   b. Guide Juniors in forming helpful habits of personal devotion.
      Use *A Year of Meetings for Junior Societies*.
      Suggest *A Child's Quiet Hour*, Emily Williston.
         Thoughts of God for Boys and Girls.
   c. Take up Foreign Mission Study.
      (See Missionary Education Announcement of Books, Maps, Plays, Pictures and other Teaching Material for 1937–1938.)

d. Observe Christian Endeavor Week; invite parents to the meetings.

See "*For Christ and the Church*," a two weeks' unit by Mrs. William V. Martin.

NOTE the unit, *The Junior and Prayer*, by Mrs. Inez D. Jayne.

Junior Christian Endeavor Topics:

2. Learning Worship from Others. Ps. 100 : 1–5. (Consecration Meeting.)
9. The Heavenly Father and His Son. John 3 : 16–18.
16. How Can We Get the Best Results from Worship? Matt. 6 :6; Ex. 19 : 10, 11.
23. "Come, Let Us Worship!" Ps. 95 : 1–11.
30. What Our Church Expects of Its Juniors. Mark 12 : 30, 31.

FEBRUARY

TRAINING IN CHRISTIAN CITIZENSHIP (We serve Him loyally in our country).

a. Emphasize the Pledge; help the Juniors to understand and live up to it.
b. Develop Christian attitudes in daily responsibilities.

Give Christian motive to citizenship training in public school program.

c. Educate and motivate for abstinence from liquor and tobacco.

(See *Children and the Alcohol Problem*, list of materials, American Baptist Publication Society.)

Suggest *Answers to Alcohol*, L. H. Caldwell, Wichita, Kansas.

NOTE: *Keeping Our Balance*, Eva Taylor (Cokesbury Press).
Helping Juniors Meet the Problem of Alcohol, teaching unit by E. K. Battle (Cokesbury Press).

NOTE: *Exploring Our Neighborhood*, Mildred M. Eakin (Abingdon Press); undated unit, Juniors and Industrial Problems, Edna May Baxter, in *Children and Labor Problems* from the Congregational Publishing Society.

Also, Pupils' Work Books:

1. *Under the Church Flag;*
2. *In Anybody's Town.*

Junior Society Topics:

6. How Can Our Society Be the Best Possible Society? 1 Cor. 12 : 14–27. (Consecration Meeting.)
13. What Things Should We Be Proud of in Our Country? Ps. 33 : 12–22.
20. What Things Should We Be Sorry for in Our Country? Isa. 5 : 11, 12, 20–23.
27. Living as Christian Citizens. Matt. 22 : 15–22.

MARCH

TRAINING IN CHURCH LOYALTY (We learn to know Him in the church).
 a. Cultivate appreciation and wholehearted participation in the services and work of the church.
 b. Co-operate in the evangelistic program of the church.
     Prepare Juniors for church membership; nurture new members.
     Give every Junior an opportunity to decide for Christ.
     (Suggest undated unit, *What It Means to Decide for Jesus*, from the Methodist Board of Education.)
     Recruit new members for church and society.
 c. Observe the Birthday of Junior Endeavor (March 29, 1883).
     (See story of first Junior Society by Mrs. Francis E. Clark, in unit, "*For Christ and the Church*," by Mrs. William V. Martin.)

NOTE: *Evangelism and Church Membership Among Juniors*, American Baptist Publication Society.

Junior Christian Endeavor Topics:
   6. The First Christian Church. Acts 2:41–47. (Consecration Meeting.)
  13. Letters to the Churches. I Cor. 1:1–6.
  20. Great Leaders of the Church. Acts 7:54–60.

NOTE: *See These Banners Go*, Frank Mead (Bobbs Merrill Company).

  27. "Living Stones." I Peter 2:1–10.

APRIL

TRAINING IN RESPONSIBILITY (We learn to know Him in the church).
 a. Complete Mission Study and activities.
 b. Strive to attain goals set.
 c. Provide for representation at conventions and conferences.

Junior Christian Endeavor Topics:
   3. Health Problems in the Country. Luke 4:31–44. (Consecration Meeting.)
  10. School Life in the Country. Prov. 3:1–9.
  17. How People Work Together in the Country. Luke 10:30–35.
  24. Making Religion Real in the Country. Matt. 18:2–6.
Series based on *Out in the Country*, Hazel V. Orton.

NOTE unit, *Easter*, Margaret D. Edwards (Pilgrim Press).

MAY

TRAINING IN CO-OPERATION (We share Him with the world).
a. Honor the Parents.
b. Cultivate attitudes of appreciation of the worth and contributions of other groups and nations; afford practice in sharing their greatest possession with others everywhere.

NOTE: *Creating a World of Friendly Children*, from the Committee on World Friendship Among Children.

c. Send reports to the State Christian Endeavor Union.

Junior Christian Endeavor Topics:
1. Stories and Poems We Love. Luke 15 : 11–24. (Consecration Meeting.)
8. Pictures We Love. Matt. 13 : 3–9.
15. Hymns and Music We Love. Luke 2 : 8–14.
22. Bible Characters We Love. Ruth 1 : 6–18.

NOTE: *Bible Autobiographies*, Mrs. Francis E. Clark (International Society of Christian Endeavor).
Bible Miniatures, Amos R. Wells (Revell).

29. Using the Things We Love. Acts 8 : 26–39.

NOTE: *Music, Poetry, and Pictures in the Christian Education of Juniors*, (American Baptist Publication Society).
Developing Appreciation through Pictures, Poems and Music in the Junior Department, (United Christian Missionary Society).

JUNE

TRAINING IN LEADERSHIP (We learn to know Him in the church).
a. Urge "growing leadership."
(Use *Growth in Christian Service*, The International Council of Religious Education.)
b. Send representatives to conventions and conferences.
c. Plan program for the summer months.
(Read and save Summer Activities for Children, Sarah E. Green, in *The Elementary Magazine* for May, 1937.)

NOTE: *Camping and Guidance*, Ernest G. Osborne (Association Press).

Junior Christian Endeavor Topics:
5. What Are the Best Books for Juniors? Ps. 119 : 9–16. (Consecration Meeting.)
12. Getting Good from the Movies. Matt. 6 : 19–23.
19. Getting Good from the Radio. Prov. 23 : 12; Rev. 5 : 11–13.
26. Choosing Only the Best. Josh. 24 : 14, 15.

JULY AND AUGUST

TRAINING IN THE WISE USE OF LEISURE TIME

a. Include outdoor recreation, constructive work, collections, nature study, dramatization and service activities.

b. Anticipate needs of individual Juniors with appropriate books and magazines; co-operate with parents, public school, librarian, and Sunday Church School to raise standards.

c. Encourage regular attendance upon all services.

d. Arrange for an Echo Meeting, when the delegates to conventions and conferences may report.

e. Consider new plans, suggested by delegates, at once.

Junior Christian Endeavor Topics:

   3. Giving My Best for My Country. Rom. 13 : 1–10. (Consecration Meeting.)

   10. Heroes of Missions in Other Lands. Acts 16 : 19–35.

   17. Heroes of Missions in America. Rom. 10 : 9–15.

   24. Brave Men and Women. Dan. 5 : 1–9, 13, 25–28.

   31. Good Things I Have Learned from Others. John 1 : 35–46.

For this series, such books as Basil Mathews' *Book of Missionary Heroes*, Archer's *Heroes of Peace*, and Niebuhr's *Greatness Passing By* are suggested.

August   7. The Promised Land. Gen. 17 : 1–8; Josh. 1 : 1–8.

   14. Where Jesus Lived as a Boy. Luke 2 : 39–52.

   21. Why the Jordan Is a Famous River. Mark 1 : 4–11.

   28. People of the Holy Land. Luke 4 : 38–44.

For this series, *Footprints in Palestine* by Madeleine S. Miller and *A Life of Jesus* by Basil Mathews are suggested.

NOTE undated units from the Methodist Board of Education:
The Use of Leisure Time.
Discovering God in Nature.

SPECIAL NOTE: The units and topics, suggested by the Sub-committee on Junior Topics of the Committee on Religious Education of Children of the International Council of Religious Education, are available in some of the denominational periodicals. The Junior Epworth League units and topics appear in *The Elementary Magazine.*

XIII

Our Resolutions

THE Thirty-sixth International Convention of Christian Endeavor finds no fitting words to express its feelings regarding
the welcome, the overflowing hospitality, the enthusiasm, the
complete and perfect arrangements, the air-cooled auditorium,
and of all arrangements at Grand Rapids. We have been deeply
moved by the splendor of your untiring efforts to make this gathering of Christian youth at this hour of crisis an outstanding event
in religious history. Be it resolved,

We extend our sincere thanks to the City Commission of Grand
Rapids for innumerable courtesies, and to the City Manager and
the Convention Bureau for invaluable help in all arrangements.

We recognize the kindness of the Chief of Police and all the
members of his department. The friendliness and patience of all
policemen have been a matter of frequent comment.

No resolution can adequately interpret our gratitude to Mr.
George Veldman and his truly great Convention Committee which
labored incessantly for two long years. The efficiency is beyond
praise. They have been worthy hosts of a worthy city. We do
not forget every member of every sub-committee. Their service
is enshrined in our memory.

We have admired the perfection of the paging, the loveliness of
the ushering, the patience of those at the registration and information desks.

The music has been a delight, and the conductors, organist, and
pianists have never been surpassed. We thank Homer Rodeheaver
for his leadership, his singing, his trombone, and especially for
himself. The pageant on Saturday night left an indelible impression.

The parade on Saturday was a memorable spectacle. It was a
demonstration of marching Christian youth, unafraid and exultant,
and we salute the marshal and all who labored for its success.

We know these convention results would have been impossible
but for the unstinted co-operation of the ministers, the churches,
and other religious organizations.

A special word is certainly due to station WOOD for exceptional
service placed at our disposal.

The far-reaching influence of the Convention has been multiplied
by the service of the *Grand Rapids Press*, the *Grand Rapids Herald*,
the *Detroit News*, and other newspaper service. They have carried
our message and story over the country, and their editorials have
faithfully interpreted our spirit.

Especially we thank the officers and members of the Grand Rapids and Michigan Christian Endeavor Unions.

The speakers and conference leaders have informed our minds and rekindled and stimulated our faith.

To Grand Rapids, its citizens, its churches, its Endeavorers, we record our praise and thanks. You have made religious history for Christian youth. Grand Rapids will always be associated with our motto, "Christ for the Crisis."

*   *   *

We are thankful to God for the clarion call of President Poling's presidential address with its high purpose and ringing challenge sounded in no uncertain terms.

We welcome the encouraging news concerning the steady forward march of Christian Endeavor around the world in many lands, and we enthusiastically greet the report that there are more state Christian Endeavor field secretaries than ever before in the history of the movement. This, we believe, bespeaks the vitality and consecration of Christian Endeavorers who are eager to be at work for God and for the uplifting of all mankind.

We urge state unions, county organizations, and local societies to be ever mindful of the financial pressure under which the International Society operates, and we urge members and friends of Christian Endeavor everywhere to make sacrificial gifts to the international organization, upon whose leadership and basic work the entire movement so largely depends.

We heartily endorse the new *Christian Endeavor World* as the official organ of the International Society, and we trust that Endeavorers everywhere will not only take seriously their responsibility and privilege to be subscribers to this essential periodical, but also that Endeavorers will do their utmost to see that suggestions, plans, inspirational and devotional materials included in the magazine bear fruit in action and practice through the length and breadth of the movement.

Prayerfully aware of the effort and consecration it will require, we accept President Poling's challenge to go from this prophetic gathering to lead a hundred thousand of our youthful associates to Jesus Christ and to enroll as many in the Quiet Hour and the Tenth Legion. Realizing the urgency of the need, can we do less? Trusting in the Lord Jesus Christ for strength, let us do as much!

We have heard from President Poling the declaration of our Chinese brother in the faith there in the face of bitter opposition and strongly entrenched adversaries, "The ultimatum to the Protestant Church is *unite or die!*" Believing that Christian Endeavor has had a God-given part in drawing the forces of Protestantism together at an ever accelerating pace in the past, we affirm our purpose to continue to be a movement demonstrating to the world that the followers of Jesus Christ in faith "are not divided, all one body we." We urge Endeavorers across denominational lines to unite in common tasks and assume joint responsibilities for the extension of the Gospel locally in America, overseas, for sometimes where different avenues of approaching God through worship may be dividing, experience has demonstrated that common avenues of co-operating with God through "work-ship" can and will bind Christian minds and hearts together in understanding and co-operative effort. Let us rejoice in being co-workers with God and through Him co-workers with each other in unity of heart and singleness of purpose.

We feel with Daniel Poling that this is an hour of tremendous crisis in world affairs. We sense, however, that it is also a crisis of significant opportunity for Christian witness and discipleship in all the areas of life. We glimpse among the threatening clouds the emerging figure of the Master of all crises, the Christ of God. The great Preaching Mission of our land indicated by its radiant progress across America the yearning of men and women to know Him "whose name is above all names." We respond with joy and enthusiasm to this appeal, and pledge our unfaltering allegiance to make this call the charter of our individual society and union life through the years as we return home from this mountain-top experience at Grand Rapids.

*   *   *

We reaffirm our faith in the saving grace of Jesus Christ unto men and nations, and that the great missionary enterprise of the Christian Church is the heart of the progress of the Kingdom of God. We desire to work for a community of peoples and nations with the spirit of Christ as the source of inspiration and bond of unity and as a control in all activities of personal living and matters of national affairs. "Christ for the Crisis" finds its grandest expression in our lives when we would "make Christ known and His way of life possible to all mankind."

*   *   *

As Christian Endeavorers, we are deeply concerned in the welfare of children. Our attention has been vividly drawn to the terrible suffering of children on both sides in war-torn Spain. We would not add to the violence or intensify the hatred. We believe in a kingdom of love in which there is no room for hatred and no mean indifference to human suffering. We heartily endorse and encourage all Endeavorers to co-operate with the non-partisan Child Feeding Mission of the American Friends Service Committee. We join with all Christian youth in this practical service.

We also desire to express our sympathy for suffering children of the Southern Mountains under conditions existing there, and commend to all societies the work of the "Save the Children Fund." We ever feel the call of the Master, "Suffer the little children to come unto Me."

*   *   *

Resolved, that we view with alarm the widespread commercialization of the Sabbath Day by those who would rob us of its blessings and privileges, as well as the indifference with which the Day is observed by many of those within our Christian fellowship. And we would call upon Christian Endeavorers and Christian people everywhere to combat vigorously every effort which seeks further to destroy and commercialize the Lord's Day. The command given centuries ago still has for us its compelling power. "Remember the Sabbath Day to keep it holy."

*   *   *

Whereas the Christian Endeavor movement since its inception has devoted itself to the cause of peace and the freeing of youth and humanity from the thraldom of war and still believes with passionate conviction that peace on earth is the imperative will of God; and

Whereas this Convention listened to the challenging call to promote peace from the lips of Admiral Byrd, one of the most distinguished of living Americans, especially remembering his words that the ideals of youth shall be amply justified in the future of their manhood and womanhood; and

Whereas the state of armed attention in which the world is living and the frenzied rearmament of the nations threaten the world with catastrophe;

Be it therefore resolved, that this Thirty-Sixth International Convention of Christian Endeavor calls upon the peoples of the world to urge their governments to disassociate themselves from war as an instrument of international policy. A solemn obligation for peace should be as binding as an obligation for war. We deplore the vast expenditures on armaments draining the wealth and resources of the world, even our own government's unprecedented outlays, diverting funds from needed civil and educational enterprises. We trust that some courageous leader will soon call the nations to a disarmament conference.

We rejoice that our own government has pursued with such striking success a good neighbor policy on this continent. We are grateful for the Christian leadership of our Secretary of State, the Honorable Cordell Hull, and trust it will be extended to other nations.

There are delegates in large numbers at this Convention from

Canada. We are proud beyond expression that along the 4000-mile borderline from the Atlantic to the Pacific, there is not a gun, not a fort, not a soldier. A treaty signed one hundred twenty-one years ago has never been broken, and, please God, it never will.

We hope that the time will speedily come when the frontier to the south will be identical in this respect and that all people will find security in unfortified frontiers.

We wholeheartedly support the policy to keep our country out of war, and we strongly feel that we can help in this by keeping war out of the world. We will urge co-operation with like-minded nations to make this a warless world

We reiterate our determination expressed at Philadelphia when we created our Department of Peace and shall continue to crusade for peace. Held to this high purpose but with feet on the ground, we pledge our support to every worthy constructive agency working for conciliation, arbitration, conference, understanding, and friendship.

As we study the causes of war we shall seek to remove the friction and injustice which breed the spirit and tragedy of war.

We desire our mighty youth movement to circle the world in a golden chain of friendship and peace.

We shall therefore educate for peace; we shall work for peace, and above all we shall pray for peace, believing in the prayer of our Lord, "Blessed are the peacemakers, for theirs is the Kingdom of Heaven."

This is our faith, the faith of Christian youth, and we shall hold high the torch of that faith until it finally and completely triumphs.

*   *   *

We are thankful for the growing sentiment against depriving human beings of life without the due processes of law, and we recognize the awakening of the Christian conscience on this matter. We shall favor strengthening the state and national legislation towards the elimination of lynching.

The Christian Endeavor movement since its inception has always opposed the traffic in beverage alcohol. It lifted the banner for a saloonless nation at one of its early conventions, and rejoiced when the national prohibition amendment was passed and our flag floated over land in which there was no legal saloon. It believes that repeal has tragically failed and that today the menace of liquor in new and insidious forms threatens the best and basic factors in American life.

We feel, in the words of President Poling's address, that the rising tides of liquor consumption, law violation, juvenile delinquency are sweeping toward a social and moral disaster. We still believe in total abstinence from alcoholic liquor, and shall prosecute with increasing vigor our campaign for this result.

We call all Endeavorers, all Endeavor Unions to an increased program of temperance education, and advocate the passage of temperance legislation and anti-liquor advertising bills, working through such activities as Allied Youth.

We pledge all the resources, all the passion of Christian Endeavor to the struggle to produce a sober people.

*   *   *

This Convention assembled in the Grand Rapids Auditorium, believes that the transforming of our world into the Kingdom of God can only be accomplished by transformed lives. The Christian program will fail unless buttressed by Christian character. We have seen, however, especially in our conferences, that Christian discipleship carries with it implications for social conduct. We dare not give to Him our allegiance on these mountain-top experiences and deny Him the same allegiance in the conduct of life when it meets pagan and brutalizing prejudices and injustices. We do not believe that there are two gospels, one social and the other individual. There is only one gospel, the Gospel of our Lord and Saviour, and it carries inescapable challenges for individual, social, and national life. We lift our voices against everything that mars and sears the personalities of men and women, destroys the home by unjust economic pressures, takes the light and happy joy from child life, and denies God's free men and women the rights of developing and pursuing life's highest usefulness. We protest against racial discrimination and injustice and against all attempts to raise barriers of prejudice between races, nationalities, and classes.

Some of our convention delegations come from Canada, and we rejoice with them in the free, ordered liberty granted to them full and unmeasured in their free institutions. The majority of the membership of this mighty throng come from states in this American Union. We highly resolve again to state our faith in the institutions of America. We believe with President Poling that neither Communism or Fascism has a place in our corporate life, but we believe and here say with ringing declaration that all change necessary to meet new situations can be fully and completely met within the constitution of our beloved land. We are aware of many imperfections in our national life. We realize that modern civilization has within it so much that is unchristian and pagan. We deplore the evils that arise out of our exaggerated national consciousness. At the same time we profess our patriotic faith in our country, its liberal form of government, its cherished civil and religious liberties, its free institutions, and its measure of moral enlightenment. We humbly believe that it represents the best there is in the world. We pledge our allegiance to a nation that honors the names of Washington and Lincoln, and we pray that our country may ever be "the land of the free and the home of the brave."

*   *   *

This body being mindful that it is but one of many similar bodies going to make up the World's Christian Endeavor Union, and recognizing the fact that our beloved president is also the beloved president of Christian Endeavorers throughout the world, is at this time particularly conscious of their deep interest in us as we assemble here and also of our sincere interest in them and their work.

Therefore, be it resolved, that this Thirty-Sixth International Convention of Christian Endeavor meeting at Grand Rapids, Michigan, in these United States of America, extends to all Christian Endeavorers throughout the world our heartiest greetings and best wishes that all may be more fruitful for the Kingdom of God than ever before.

*   *   *

This Thirty-Sixth International Convention of Christian Endeavor held at Grand Rapids, Michigan, July 8 to 13, 1937, having heard with keenest delight President Poling read the call to the World's Convention to be held in Melbourne, Australia, in August, 1938, pledges itself in every way to work towards making this one of the most successful gatherings of Christian youth in modern times. It assures the Australian Endeavorers that the Endeavorers of America will do all within their power to be represented by an adequate delegation.

*   *   *

Whereas President Poling in his address said, "Following Grand Rapids, our next great convention landmark is Melbourne, Australia, August 2 to 8, 1938—next summer. The Australian national committee is composed of a remarkable group of men and women, representative of both church life and public affairs. Plans already made have more generously regarded the needs of the World's Christian Endeavor Union than those of any other similar gathering. It is our earnest hope that a representative delegation will go out to Australia from the United States and that there may be a large general movement from all other countries. This will be the first international gathering of our society ever held in Australia."—

Be it resolved, that those attending this convention rejoice in the remarkable reception and welcome given to President Poling by the Endeavorers of Australia, are thrilled by their remarkable progress and achievements, are happy their land is to be host of the next World's Convention, and will do their utmost to secure a worthy delegation from the United States and contribute to what promises to be one of the most historic and significant gatherings of Christian youth in our generation.

*   *   *

We, the members of this Thirty-Sixth International Convention, desire to place on record our profound thankfulness to God for the presence (in our midst) of Mrs. Francis E. Clark, affectionately known to us all as Mother Clark. Her gentle, radiant Christian witness through the entire fifty-six years of Christian Endeavor history has been a torch lighting the way for millions in all lands. We think of her beloved husband, our unforgotten founder, and we pray that as she witnesses our unbroken devotion to his high purpose, she may again see the fulfillment of that immortal truth, "To live in the hearts of those we love is not to die."

We salute Mother Clark with affection too great for expression. She is the one unbroken link of Christian Endeavor history, and we pledge to her our love as she gives to us again the inspiration of her presence and the ripe, rich wisdom of her experience

XIV

Who's Who in the

GRAND RAPIDS CONVENTION COMMITTEE
Thirty-Sixth International
Christian Endeavor Convention

EXECUTIVE COMMITTEE

General Chairman, George Veldman
Associate Chairman, Lester C. Doerr
Vice-Chairman, Lawrence D. Beukema
Vice-Chairman, Russell J. Boyle
Vice-Chairman, Fred P. Geib
Vice-Chairman, H. Fred Oltman

Vice-Chairman, Frank V. Smith
Secretary, Mrs. M. J. Van Ess
Treasurer, Clifford Buchanan
State Secretary, Ernest S. Marks
National Secretary, Carroll M. Wright
President G. R. Union, Carroll Herlein

COMMITTEE CHAIRMEN

Automobile, George Vruggink
Badges, Armen S. Kurkjian
Banquet, Clare B. Krenz
Communion Service, Rev. John H. Meengs
Decorations—Halls, Fred Speckin
Exhibits, Charles W. Puehl
Finance, Howard C. Lawrence
Hotels and Housing, Gladys Cameron, John Hendrickson, Jr.
Information, Marion Siekman
Intermediate, Richard Winters
Junior, Mrs. J. C. Muste
Literature, Marshall Rector

Music, John R. Klaasse
Pages and Guides, Mrs. John H. Rietberg
Parade, Mallery M. Kincaid
Press—Publicity, Peter Verburg
Program, Henry W. Walstrom
Promotion, Carroll Herlein
Pulpit Supply, Rev. J. A. Dykstra, D.D.
Radio, Stanley W. Barnett
Reception, Herman W. Verseput
Registration— City, Albert Van Dyke
Registration—State, Harold J. Becker
Ushers, Mrs. C. E. Edwards

MINISTERIAL ASSOCIATION COMMITTEE

Rev. Edward P. Downey, *Chairman*, Westminster Presbyterian Church
Rev. Raymond R. Brown, Griggs Street Evangelical Church
Rev. Lester A. Kilpatrick, D.D., First Methodist Church
Rev. Edward Masselink, Ph.D., Burton Heights Christian Reformed Church
Rev. Milton M. McGorrill, D.D., Fountain Street Baptist Church

Rev. Bernard J. Mulder, D.D., Reformed Church
Rev. LeRoy T. Robinson, D.D., Trinity M. E. Community Church
Rev. Harold N. Skidmore, South Congregational Church
Rev. Ralph J. White, D.D., Trinity English Lutheran Church

ADVISORY COMMITTEE

Leland S. Westerman, *Chairman*, General Secretary Y.M.C.A.

John W. Blodgett, Prominent Civic Leader

125

Dr. Henry Beets, *Secretary*, Christian Reformed Mission Board

Hon. John A. Collins, Mayor, East Grand Rapids

L. J. DeLamarter, General Manager, Grand Rapids Railroad Company

Miss Marie A. Gezon, Head of Girls' Guidance Department, City of Grand Rapids

Louis H. Grettenberger, Assistant City Attorney

Armen S. Kurkjian, Sales Manager, Oliver Machinery Co.

Clay H. Hollister, President, Old Kent Bank

Hon. Tunis Johnson, Mayor, Grand Rapids

Hon. Carl E. Mapes, Representative in Congress, Fifth District

John P. Otte, President, American Laundry

Rev. Melvin E. Trotter, Superintendent, City Rescue Mission

Hon. Arthur H. Vandenberg, United States Senator

John Van Den Berg, Van Den Berg Furniture Company

Dr. Paul G. Voelker, Former State Superintendent of Public Instruction

Mrs. Raymond G. Zwingeberg, former President, Federation of Women's Clubs

The above shows only the various Committee Chairmen. They were assisted by a great corps of able and loyal workers. It is by reason of the combined efforts of the Officers, Committee Chairmen, and members that this Convention is made possible.

BOOK 2

"The very first One Hundred Registrations for Grand Rapids Appeared in an Honor-roll, and Served as an Incentive for the 1939 Convention"

MR. VELDMAN PRESENTS THE HONOR-ROLL TO DR. POLING

*A Program Guide**

for Christian Endeavor Societies and Interdenominational Unions

THE Program of Objectives for Christian Endeavor societies and unions, adopted and released by the officers and the Board of Trustees of the International Society of Christian Endeavor at the Grand Rapids Convention, puts into practical application, for society and union work, the spirit and purpose of Christian Endeavor's new commitment—*Christ for the Crisis.*

Alongside these special objectives and woven into them are the salient features of the United Christian Youth Program, with its covering title, "Christian Youth Building a New World."

But undergirding all these special and changing goals are the unchanging principles of Christian Endeavor, likewise the divisions and department of its work which go on from year to year— personal allegiance to Christ; evangelism; Bible study; daily devotions, including the Quiet Hour; stewardship, including the enrollment of members of the Tenth Legion; church loyalty; missions; Christian citizenship. All these things together provide challenges to the hosts of young people who endeavor for Christ and the church.

Section I

Christ for Every Crisis in Personal Living

(A vital, personal religion sufficient for every personal need.)

A. A personal decision to accept Jesus Christ as Saviour and Lord.
   1. Re-emphasis. on that principle of Christian Endeavor which calls every active member of the society to be openly committed to Christ and to the Christian life.

From Convention Messages

Jesus Christ has, Jesus Christ is, the only solution for the world's problems. And He is so complete and powerful. He Himself is so entirely adequate, that eventually, in spite of all our divisions, in spite of all our failures, He will complete the salvation of the world. In Him is our unity. Color, language, race, nations, and denominations divide us. But all colors, all races, all tongues, all nations, and all denominations are at last of the one blood of His eternal covenant.

*Founded on A Program of Objectives, adopted by the Board of Trustees. International Society of Christian Endeavor, supplemented by material presented at the Convention Conferences by 45 leaders. Edited by Bert H. Davis.

Nor is our belief in Him a mere intellectual affirmation. It is revolution. It is a new man and a new woman. It is the regeneration of the individual, of individual practice, and of society itself. It is the New Birth, a birth as mysterious as the coming of a new life into the world and *more* profound.

—*Daniel A. Poling*

Real Christianity is that to which baffled, frustrated people should be able to turn as thirsty men to a deep, cool spring where invigorating waters flow. Our fathers knew the art of spiritual power and harnessed it to their lives and to society. . . .

Great power is available to the person who learns to trust God completely, that is, utterly to rest his life with all of its problems and burdens on God. Alas, most of us do not have faith of this variety. We mumble a creed, live more or less respectable lives, and think we are people of faith, which we are not. Real faith is inevitably associated with lives of power and effectiveness.

—*Norman Vincent Peale*

Intermediates' Statements in Conference

To me it seems that three-fourths of the people who are supposed to be Christians do not take the standards seriously.

Some churches are fashionable to attend; it is the thing to do because of the various other persons who belong.

Because the standards are low, people keep them low. If they were raised, people would strive to achieve them.

Great Affirmations of Faith

These are illustrative of the great affirmations of Christian faith and belief: God, Jesus Christ, the Holy Spirit, Love, Forgiveness, Man, World, Immortality, Church, Sacraments. We cannot know all there is to be known about each or all of these and others, but the important thing is to let what we do know have outlet and influence in our lives.

What sources have young people for the discovery and enhancement of their affirmations of faith? Largely a matter of personal experience through contact with others, reading, observation. Use the laboratory method of trying out some of our Christian affirmations and see what a difference they make in life. What special helps come from church, Scriptures, church history, teachings of Christians of our own day?

There will be difficulties. Personal friends are not sympathetic. Zeal dies down, when one is farther away from a great experience.

We need to engage in personal friendships which are in accord with our own ideals of Christian living. We need to relate our ideals and affirmations to God through personal and public worship. We need to develop a personal technique which gives us satisfaction and strength to be a Christian. We need to "live so that others will love us." This may sound selfish, but if we think it through, love is inspired by its own kind, which is love.

—*Albert J. Anthony*

To Measure the Christian

There are at least four measures by which a Christian may be appraised. The first is complete loyalty to Christ, no matter what the cost. The second, a constant contact with the sources of spiritual power. Then the application of Jesus' spirit and teaching to those difficulties that seem to make one man the enemy of another. Fourth, the Christian will challenge others to follow Christ, and also will build an enduring loyalty to the church, formed of those who follow Him.

Loyalty to Christ is demonstrated in everyday living, by exemplifying honesty, unselfishness, purity and love.

--Frank D. Getty

How Societies Help

Church attendance. In many societies, every member will accept seriously the challenge to attend the church services regularly. Attendance records may be kept. The pastor should be in touch with the percentages reached.

Devotional meetings. To be held throughout the year, including summer months. Members loyally accepting the responsibilities of leading meetings, participation, singing and special features. Observance of New Year's Eve, an Easter sunrise meeting, a "going away" devotional meeting with members leaving for school and college as guests, and a monthly consecration meeting are other desirable activities of the society.

Prayer groups. Often these will meet before the regular weekly devotional meeting. At some seasons, as preceding Easter, neighborhood prayer groups might meet, with the evangelistic work of the church and society especially in mind.

Also see Section II-D.

B. Growth in Christian living through participation in the active enterprises of the Kingdom.

1. The society vigorously enrolling Comrades of the Quiet Hour for daily devotions, and promoting a fresh study of the Holy Scriptures as indispensable for Christian living.

2. Continual emphasis on the principle of loyalty to the church, especially regular attendance at the worship services on the part of all Endeavorers, and active participation in the several divisions of the church's program of work.

3. The society enlisting tithers and enrolling them as members of the Tenth Legion.

4. The society promoting an energetic campaign for reading only the best literature—in books, magazines and newspapers; for choosing only such radio programs, moving pictures, and other diversions as will make positive contributions to character-building and religious development.

5. Encouraging young people to be definite in their Christian service, with commitment to specific activities, both in the society and in the church.

For the Quiet Hour

Quiet Hour Comrades individually agree to this pledge: "Trusting in the Lord Jesus Christ for strength, I will make it the rule of my life to set apart at least fifteen minutes every day, if possible in the early morning, for quiet meditation and direct communion with God."

Some Comrades desire to record with the society, the local union, and the International Society of Christian Endeavor the statement that they have entered into this daily practice. Frequently, leaders hear from some Alumni Endeavorer who has been keeping such a covenant for a long span of years and rejoices in the experience.

How Develop Devotional Life?

How shall we develop our love for Jesus Christ?
First, by letting Him talk to us through our consciences and through the Bible.
Second, by talking to Him through the means of prayer.
Third, by our work of love for Christ.
Memorizing the Scriptures is important, but we should learn discriminately—finding and memorizing the verse that speaks to us on a great subject and putting this into the quiver of our spiritual resources.
We should be careful not to become selfish in our prayers. It is important that we widen the horizons of our prayers. Let them be chiefly for others.

—John R. Mulder

A Technique for Prayer

(Based on Matthew 6 : 6)

1. A period—"When thou prayest . . . "
2. A place—"Enter into thine inner chamber . . . "
3. A privacy—"Shut thy door   "
4. A poise—"Pray to thy Father who is in secret."
5. A promise—"Thy Father which seeth in secret shall recompense thee."

Recommended as devotional reading: "Follow Me," monthly worship guide for daily devotions, Presbyterian Board of Christian Education; "The Fellowship of Prayer," Lenten booklet distributed annually by the Federal Council of the Churches of Christ in America; Fosdick, "The Meaning of Prayer"; Foulkes, "Youthways to Life"; Muriel Lester, "Ways of Praying"; Willett, "The Daily Altar."

—Raymond M. Veh

Around the Week in Prayer

GOD IS—
  Sunday. Joy. Read Heb. 1 : 9; John 15 : 11; Phil. 4 : 4; Deut. 12 : 7.
  Monday. Life. John 10 : 10; Rev. 22 : 17; Gal. 2 : 20; Mark 16 : 15, 18; John 7 : 23; Mark 11 : 24.
  Tuesday. Power. Rev. 19 : 6; Gen. 17 : 1; Acts 1 : 8; Phil. 4 : 13.
  Wednesday. Light. I John 1 : 5; John 8 : 12; Eph. 5 : 8; Ps. 16 : 11; Matt. 5 : 16.
  Thursday. Love. I John 4 : 7, 11; Eph. 5 : 1; I Cor. 13 : 4, 11.
  Friday. The Cross. John 3 : 16; John 12 : 32; John 17 : 20, 23; Luke 9 : 23; I Pet. 2 : 19, 25.
  Saturday. Peace. Phil. 4 : 7; Matt. 5 : 9; Phil. 4 : 6; I Pet. 5 : 7; John 14 : 27.

—Mrs. Daniel A. Poling

Five Claims of Stewardship

1. Stewardship claims priority in one's life.
2. Stewardship claims the right to the best one has.
3. Stewardship claims the right to recognition in all increase that might come.

4. Stewardship lays claim to regularity.

5. Stewardship lays claim to universality.

Stewardship is "being responsible for the direction and use of something that belongs to another." Our talents belong to God, and we are responsible for their use. This is fundamental to all religions.

Many do not think of stewardship from the standpoint of *time*. On the average, twenty hours out of the 168-hour week are absolutely lost from actual activity. Young people can come to see that this time can be organized so that they will have opportunity to do things which they are not now doing.

We must have a schedule, organizing our time so that the Lord can have the proper amount of our service. Almost every church is begging for people who are willing to assist. —*E. E. Harris*

How Societies Help

Seasonal Emphases. Simultaneously with the presentation of certain appropriate topics or groups of topics, the enrollment of Comrades of the Quiet Hour may be promoted, quietly and with dignity. Another favorable time for such enrollment is between Thanksgiving Day and New Year's Day, in preparation for a new daily practice for the new year. Also in Lent, the practice being associated with the use of the Federal Council's "Fellowship of Prayer." Denominations will aid societies to choose a time and a method for enrolling those practicing stewardship of time, talents, and money as Tenth Legion members.

Tenth Legion Covenant. "As a Christian whose practice it is to dedicate one-tenth or more of my income to the Lord's work, you will please enroll me in the Tenth Legion."

Church Loyalty. The officers of the society should be prepared to give a good example in attendance, activity, and dependability, with reference to their church obligations in total. The Christian Endeavor society lives to strengthen and serve the church.

See also II-A, II-B and II-C.

How Unions Help

Good Literature. The union may post the names of worthy, carefully chosen books, or make such books available through a loan library or a book club. Occasionally a union's monthly meeting may feature the reviews of good books that members have read. A society might represent in drama or pageantry some book or periodical of unusual worth. Keep in touch with the movies recommended by character-building agencies and in some of the religious periodicals (including *The Christian Century* and *Epworth Herald*) Unions will not seek to promote movie attendance, but may have available for pastors and societies the lists that such groups have prepared on films likely to be presented locally.

Enrollments. Unions may name certain weeks or months in which each society is requested to present such causes as the Quiet Hour and Tenth Legion. In planning for addresses, conferences, and union publications, the importance of these enrollments—which carry out obligations already inherent in the Christian Endeavor pledge or covenant—may be mentioned and they may be fully explained.

C. Frequent and regular testimony, both by word and by deed, as to the Christian experience; sharing with others through conversation and through other methods of approach the good results of faith and experience.

1. The society giving encouragement in its meetings to all young people to speak in testimony of their experience.

Better Devotional Meetings

A conference led by *Herbert L. Minard* considered purposes of the devotional meeting to be: Christian fellowship, worship, inspiration for Christian living.

These are problems in Christian living: Tendency to "follow the crowd," how to demonstrate to others that the Christian life is worth while, discovering and using one's talents to the best advantage.

Those of the group are often able to help one another in these matters. Encourage a frank expression of needs and doubts. Let those of more experience, the society's counselor included, share their ideas and experiments that have touched these very points of questioning and difficulty.

Worship, Fellowship, Counsel

Among objectives for the devotional meeting are: Development of expression, seeking outcomes of service and action, securing values of Christian fellowship, participating in experiences and values of group worship, establishing examples of Christian living, training for church leadership, seeking together the Christian interpretation and solution of common problems.

The discussions should be kept practical, within young people's range of interest and information. Present "cases," seeking the group's interpretations of the Christian way to deal with them. A problem of life may be borrowed from motion picture, book, or famous painting.

—Willard E. Rice

D. Individual and society effort to lead others to Christ.

    1. The society encouraging its members, through participation in the evangelistic plans of the church, study classes, prayer groups, personal workers' bands, win-my-friend campaigns, pre-Easter meetings, or other methods, to bring other young people to the point of definite commitment of their lives to Christ.

Means to Evangelize

Some of the methods used today in leading people to know Christ:

Street meetings, example of individual life (our own actions), distribution of Christian literature, evangelistic meetings (singly or in series), personal evangelism (making a point of contact with people you meet, through conversation), through someone you love, parents' influence with their children, assigning responsibilities to persons with a talent (interested in the church, yet not in membership).

Many refrain from any effort to evangelize because they fear some question will be asked that they cannot answer. This is largely due to unpreparedness. If we don't have the tool to meet the particular situation, we Christian Endeavorers know where to find it. Young people, indeed, are the better prepared for evangelistic work by the very fact that people do not regard them as "experts" in religion, but "enthusiasts."

There is no fanaticism about a religious enthusiasm that puts God before self. Remember that we cannot judge another's conversion by our own religious experience.

—Andrew J. Kurth

How Unions Help

Conduct a study and training course in "Winning Chums to Christ." Study together a text on soul-winning; your pastor counselors will recommend some.

Assist in keeping Christian ranks intact by being on the lookout for newcomers among young people, Christian Endeavorers and others, who enter the community. Help the newcomers to find comradeship in the churches.

E. Dependence on Christ as the most valuable aid in every personal crisis.

> 1. The society arranging for and encouraging personal counselling, using one or more experienced and trustworthy adults, to assist young people in finding help as they meet the problems of unbelief, disappointment, personal sorrow, vocational choice, standards of conduct, and the like.

From Dr. Norwood's Address

The most remorseful person is not the great sinner, but it is he who has sinned *once* and cannot forgive himself.

How Unions Help

The pastor counselors of the union will help to serve both pastors and people if they will call attention of their fellow clergymen to this section and to the readiness and expectancy which it will awake among many young people seeking advice and help.

Section II

Christ for Every Crisis in Community Life

(*The church and Christian Endeavor society concerned in every community need*)

A. Re-emphasis on the principle of membership in and loyalty to the church.

> 1. The society encouraging all its members to be active and thorough in their support of the church.
>
> 2. The society endeavoring to make the church more attractive to young people, in fellowship, education, planned activities, and spiritual emphasis.
>
> 3. The society engaging in one or more campaigns to increase church attendance.

How Societies Help

Church Attendance. The society may fill certain pews or sections at some designated services of the church. In some societies, church attendance is recorded and the rising or falling percentage of members at church is carefully watched by society officers. Participation of the members in ushering, the choir, bringing others to services, the leadership of some services, aids the church attendance efforts.

Contributions. The call of the church for its own support and for missionary objectives should be seasonally given in the society. A member of the society or a younger church officer may speak and answer questions on the subject. Christian Endeavor loyalty is not measured by contributions alone, but where the heart is, there the treasure is placed, also.

Miscellaneous Services. Teaching and substituting in the church school. Maintaining a nursery so parents of young children can attend services. Mending hymnals. Repairing and painting equipment. Caring for church grounds. Mimeographing church bulletin. Securing publicity for the church. Addressing envelopes. Making and keeping various records and files.

Endeavorers Aid the Church

1. By planning committees, promoting and conducting surveys of community needs and the church activities required to meet these.

2. By studying the teachings of the prophets and Jesus in relation to today's issues.

3. By fostering intelligent study of Christian attitudes toward personal problems.

4. By preparing to serve as instructors and leaders.

5. By sharing in "Christian Youth Building a New World."

—Raymond M. Veh

For Efficient Societies

Train the officers. Have a turn-over in leadership. Send new officers to conferences and rallies, where they can become acquainted with others doing the same work, the methods they use, the great objectives to which the whole movement is committed.

Let officers work as "representatives in leadership" of the membership of the society. What does the society think about this or that activity?

Question. What will make Christian Endeavor function?

Answer. All in all, one inspired person, with a distinctive prayer life and filled with spiritual power who really wants to, can so move and work as to cause problems to seem small, before a Higher Power.

—Robert S. Nance

B. Participation in the education and service programs of the church.

1. Strengthening the individual societies and groups through correlation of the programs and activities of all organizations for young people in the church through a representative committee on young people's work or Christian education.

2. Establishing the principle of one or more adult counselors (adviser, sponsor, coach) for every Christian Endeavor, or other young people's, society in all age groups.

3. The Christian Endeavor societies actively sharing in the total educational program in the church.

4. Providing for the effective training of all young people by the establishment of graded societies wherever practicable.
5. Establishing leadership education classes and providing for the coaching of young people so that their skills may be developed.

Christian Endeavor Council

The Christian Endeavor Council, or Committee, is advisable in a church that has three or more societies, or the possibilities for these. It consists of the president and adviser of each society, plus a chairman nominated by these representatives and elected by the official board of the church. He will be the Christian Endeavor Superintendent—his work related to the pastor and to the church board or committee on Christian education on the same terms as the Sunday School Superintendent.

The most important project of some councils is in co-operation with the pastor and the official board to perfect a general Sunday evening service program. Merged services are finding wide acceptance.

—Paul C. Brown

Society Organization

It is important that the society should have some means of linking with the other societies of the church.

Have only committees that are needed. Put the function of a committee before the structure. Better a temporary committee, active, than a permanent committee that is dead. Have specific duties for each member of each committee.

—Clifford Earle

Provide Enough Societies

Every society comes upon the problems connected with grading. The mixture of ages within a society makes it difficult to get the best results. The three-society plan should be possible in almost every church, as follows:

> *a.* Junior society, ages 9 to 12
> *b.* Intermediate society, ages 13 to 17
> *c.* Young People's society, 18 and over*

Advantages of Christian Endeavor graded topics. Experienced workers and typical Endeavorers have worked together in planning these topics and compiling helpful materials to start discussion. A well-balanced diet. These topics provide a start and give definite plans to place in the hands of the leader, but usually the exact course and outcome of discussion are not charted. Occasionally, Intermediate and Young People's topics may be "swapped." If a study book is used for discussion in devotional meetings, be sure it is one suited to the age group, equipped with suggestions for additional study and discussion (not an encyclopædia in itself!), related to young people's life interests and character needs.

—Fred L. Mintel

Sunday Evening Fellowship

Successfully operated at Warren Avenue Presbyterian Church, Saginaw, Michigan, for six years, with an average attendance of 180 for thirty-eight weeks

If five societies: Junior, 9 to 11; Intermediate, 12 to 14; Senior, 15 to 17; Young People's, 18 to 23; Fellowship (or Adult), 24 and over.

a year (September to May) is a Christian Endeavor Fellowship of seven societies. Its meeting combines the Sunday evening church service with the graded worship and discussion and leadership-training phases of the separate society meetings. A school of missions is conducted throughout November.

Schedule: 5:30 to 6:20. Seven Christian Endeavor meetings are held, the five youngest groups having adult advisers. 6:20–6:40. Closing service in the church for all, with ten-minute talk by the pastor, special musical number, and benediction. 6:40–7:10. Christian fellowship around the tables in the dining-room, all seated by age groups. No program here, except the blessing.

Refreshments are brought from the homes—sandwiches, cakes, pickles, hot cocoa or coffee. Postal card reminders are sent to those who should bring sandwiches or cake. If one or two in a family, they bring once a month; if three or more, the turn comes twice a month.

—Jonas William Boyer

How Unions Help

Christian Endeavor Training School or Institute. The conference setup and subjects of the Grand Rapids Convention may be reproduced on a reduced scale, proportionate to the size of the union and to available leadership from older Endeavorers, pastors, religious educators, laymen.

Courses in Lookout work, Missionary Committee work, Recreation leadership methods, Better Prayer-meetings, and Graded Christian Endeavor methods (as well as training in union work) are especially within the union's educational field. The union is ready to meet the training needs that its constituent societies discover are not adequately met otherwise.*

The conventions and mass meetings of the union may almost invariably include some conference and instructional opportunities for new and prospective officers and committee chairmen of societies. In connection with a mass meeting, a supper conference is sometimes planned at which the visiting speaker and other invited Christian Endeavor leaders give brief informative talks to a selected group of society presidents or other society officers and counselors, asking questions, introducing new printed helps, and seeking to analyze training needs that the union should meet in its later program.

C. Co-operation in the worship activities of the church.

   1. Continued attention paid to the use of the best methods for public and private worship.

   2. Careful use of the particular hymns, prayers, responses, poetry, meditation, symbols, and other elements to be used in worship, to the end that public meetings may be impressive and far-reaching in spiritual results, and private worship intensified.

   3. Participation in the worship services of the church, the young people occasionally being in charge.

Public Worship

The worship service provides for experiences that are far more deep and vital than listening to a lecture or watching an entertainment. It is a sublime act in

*Condensed from "Leadership through Christian Endeavor." International Society of Christian Endeavor. $1.00 (cloth).

which the entire parish, either directly or indirectly, takes part. Every one within the sanctuary and, indeed, every one who is not present but who turns his thoughts toward the house of prayer, helps the church perform its act of worship

Typical purposes in attending services of worship are: . . to seek and find the presence of God or some manifestation of God; to praise God for what He is and what He does; to express gratitude to God; to express penitence, to confess sins, to be assured of pardon and absolution; to gain strength to resist temptation, to keep clean and pure; to meditate upon things true, honorable, just, pure, and lovely; to consecrate my talents, my time, myself, to the task begun by Christ—the realization of the Kingdom of God

—Norman E. Richardson

How Unions Help

The Christian Endeavor union is frequently in charge of, or sharing in the direction of, an Easter sunrise prayer-meeting, a watch-night meeting (New Year's Eve), a united youth communion service, or similar corporate worship experiences. The best leadership and advice should be sought on such occasions so that the meeting, in spirit and in content, will demonstrate to hosts of young people what elements may well be sought in their own society and church services.

Classes in worship's elements are recommended for union study courses, particularly if there are available the services, study helps, art and music illustrations, and other definite aids that have been made available because one or more clergymen of the community have majored in the study of worship.

D. Participation in definite projects of community evangelism.

1. The society acting either by itself or with other groups to Christianize persons in the community, using such aids as vacation Bible schools, visitation, public meetings, missions, and the like.

How Unions Help

Inventory the community. Are the great masses of young people getting an opportunity to live wholesomely, enjoy healthful recreation, acquire and live up to ideals, make friends with those who have had Christian training advantages. The many needs revealed and shared with the societies and pastors will probably point toward a more intensive united evangelical program than the community's religious institutions now support.

The typical situation of the small city or the larger village summons us to: *group evangelism,* for those who can be reached by the conventional types of church program and appeal; *support of special agencies,* such as rescue missions, the Salvation Army, vacation schools, neighborhood houses (to whom voluntary help from young people is practically as essential as funds); *widened recreational programs,* in which churches and societies, Christian Associations, neighborhood houses, and other groups share ideas, personnel, facilities, and funds; *probation and rescue work* to reach young delinquents and interest them in wholesome activity; *hobby activities* to serve as the winter interests for those who play in streets and playgrounds in summer but have no wholesome, inexpensive gathering-place for cold, dark nights.

Unions should be challenging and training the leadership of the societies, particularly Christian Endeavorers in the early twenties, for such tasks as these. The society is the training-school for church leadership; the union has a similar responsibility toward the community and those agencies that are organized to improve it.

E. Active participation in the leisure-time activities of the community, with a view to their enlargement and improvement.

    1. A careful survey of the ways in which the young people of the community spend their leisure time.

    2. Establishment of recreational counter-attractions to supplant those which are detrimental to the moral and spiritual development of youth.

    3. Encouragement of constructive hobbies, cultural, creative, or recreational.

    4. Improvement of the recreational program provided for the society.

A Better Community

A local church which is vitally concerned about the affairs of its own community—that *they* be Christian—is growing members about whom we may have no fear. Their ultimate concern will be for the wider affairs and the genuine welfare of the State, the Nation, and the world.

—Albert J. Anthony

Community Leisure-Time Projects

A neighborhood amateur night, in which children or adults or both take part. An open-house night, in a host of homes, reaching those near to you. Instructions by a handicraft teacher, open to those living near your home, near the church or other center, or specially invited on the basis of possible need for such pursuits. Home and group movies. Fun with silhouettes, using a projector or taking pictures. A community rock garden on unused land. A neighborhood newspaper, if well conducted, creates a good spirit. Get a general participation in all such projects, or drop them for something more attractive.

(Sources of information: Leisure League of America, 30 Rockefeller Plaza, New York City; Co-operative Recreation Service, Delaware, Ohio.)

—Franklin J. Hinkamp

(For union suggestions, see preceding section.)

F. Co-operation in the enactment and enforcement of law in the community.

    1. The society showing intelligent concern over poorly made or poorly enforced laws, especially as they affect young people and children (e.g., those pertaining to liquor and other narcotics, those pertaining to the protection of the Sabbath day, those pertaining to salacious literature, those pertaining to gambling).

    2. The society informing itself on the issues of local government: the forces which oppose equal opportunities for all who live in the community; and taking steps to remedy discrimination, prejudice, and injustice.

3. The society participating in community efforts in behalf of underprivileged fellow men, as distinct Christian service; or, if no such efforts exist, making a start in that direction.

Refer also to Dr. Poling's address, given in full in Chapter VI.

How Unions Help

Among magazines in the religious social action and the social service world that unions can make known (sell, share, or promote): *Social Action*, published by the Council for Social Action of the Congregational and Christian Churches; *Information Service*, Federal Council of the Churches of Christ in America; *Survey Graphic*. (Ask your pastors for additional suggestions.)

Unions find Sections II-D, II-E, and II-F to be closely related. All are included within the field of widening the opportunities and privileges to benefit many who do not seek out the church and hence sometimes have been forgotten by the Christian church as a whole. That which makes Christ known in evangelism provides a more wholesome tone for the business and recreation of the community and hence makes law-breaking and delinquency less common and more surely punished. Perverting decency for private profit is a more serious concern than individual delinquency. By religion and education, the church, the society, and the union are to advance the community standards and the ideals of citizenship; by social action, organized resistance, intelligent publicity, they should be united in making commercialized evil unsafe and unprofitable to its proprietors.

See also Section I-4. The society must first inform and cultivate the tastes of its own members.

G. Participation in the work of other Christian agencies in the field of youth, especially the United Christian Youth Movement, "Christian Youth Building a New World."

Sources of Information

Your denomination or council of churches.

International Society of Christian Endeavor, 41 Mount Vernon Street, Boston, Massachusetts.

International Council of Religious Education, 203 North Wabash Avenue, Chicago, Ill.

H. Participation in community projects in church co-operation and Christian unity.

1. Supporting by membership and activity the local union of Christian Endeavor.

2. Co-operation in special campaigns for evangelism, missions, citizenship, or peace, especially where the youth field is included.

Suggestions

The union may secure by questionnaire addressed to pastors and church school superintendents information as to present or prospective societies of Christian Endeavor. It is customary for a local union to accept into membership any such society that is authorized by its church or other supporting agency (mission, neighborhood house, boarding school, Army Post, etc.) and that is faithful to the spirit of "Trusting in the Lord Jesus Christ for strength, I promise Him that I will strive to do whatever He would like to have me do

For information on forming a union where none now exists or is active, address your State Union headquarters or the International Society of Christian Endeavor, 41 Mount Vernon Street, Boston, Massachusetts.

Many church councils or federations now include in the membership of the official board or program committee the president or another representative of the local union of Christian Endeavor. This adds to the effective co-operation of the Protestant forces, youth and adult, of the community.

I. Promotion of *The Christian Endeavor World* (Official Organ of the International Society of Christian Endeavor). Monthly, $1.00 a year; in Canada, $1.50; in foreign countries, $2.00.

Appoint a Representative

Every society and union should appoint a representative to receive subscriptions to the *World* and to promote its wide use. Enroll such representatives with Mr. Carroll M. Wright, 41 Mount Vernon Street, Boston Massachusetts.

J. Establishment and promotion of a "Best Literature Campaign" in society, church and community, with the aim of avoiding trashy and inferior magazines and books, and using only the best.

Suggestions

A church school and Christian Endeavor society reading-room is one means to aid good fellowship and both entertainment and instruction through reading. A circulating library may be conducted, if local facilities are incomplete at that point. Old books and magazines, no longer put to good use in the homes, may be made available for circulation locally or in more needy areas. In some such co-operative plans, wholesome and desirable books and magazines are circulated and avidly read until they actually fall apart in use.

*   *   *   *

In general, the application of the spirit and teachings of Jesus Christ to all community needs will provide an active demonstration of Christ for Every Community Crisis.

Section III

Christ for Every Crisis in National Life

(The Christian Gospel applied to national problems)

A. Support of economic justice.

　　1. The society establishing surveys and study groups to bring about intelligent conviction on the principles, prac-

tices, and needs of the economic order; changes and improvements which may be made, the better to establish the welfare of the entire citizenship of the nation.

B. Support of racial goodwill; breaking down the barriers of prejudice.

    1. Practicing the principles of brotherhood in the church and community; leading others to understand the irrational bases of racial distrust and hatred.

    2. Studying the causes of prejudice against those of other races, nationalities, religions, or cultures, and seeking to overcome these prejudices by the application of the principles of Jesus.

    3. Encouraging local and community friendliness toward those of other races; e.g., equal school and library opportunities; equal hospitalization; equal opportunities for earning a livelihood and for carrying out the responsibilities of parenthood; equal opportunities for recreation, for protection by the law, and for moral and religious advancement.

    4. Participating in inter-racial projects; e.g., international clubs, Americanization centers, inter-racial correspondence.

    5. Co-operating in studies and projects seeking to establish understanding and brotherhood between Protestant Christians and those of other religious connection.

Facing Problems

In order to make America Christian these problems must be considered:

Alcohol. Race prejudice. Industrial conflict. Gambling. Obscene literature. False propaganda. Divorce. Sabbath observance. Hunger. Poverty. Unemployment. Public school system. Tendencies to Fascism.

The story is told of a young woman from the South who was attending an Eastern college. A devoted Christian, she really determined to discover her faults and do something about them. As she left her room, she discovered a Negro girl was rooming three doors from her. A great antipathy welled up within her. Immediately she returned to her room, dropped to her knees, and asked for courage to do what she knew was right.

After a few moments, the girl was able to go to her Negro neighbor and say: "Are you thirsty? I am. Let's go out for a soda."

This represents the first two courses of action in the remedy for social ills: Prayer with a willingness to be convicted of personal sin, and action in the reverse

Other suggestions: Study the situations as they are, in the spirit of the words, "Know the truth and the truth shall make you free." Express convictions openly; others may be waiting for your reaction and your testimony. Service—and don't be content with Thanksgiving baskets.

A practical missionary project can be carried out in any community by having a committee or person call in neighborhoods where a race problem exists, ministering sympathy, aid, Christian teaching, and "the cup of cold water."

                                            —Ruth I. Seabury

E. Continuation of the fight against alcohol and other narcotics.

    1. Promoting the principle of total abstinence from the use and sale of alcohol as a beverage, including the signing and circulation of total abstinence pledges.

    2. Supporting education concerning the unfavorable effects of alcohol, through meetings, addresses, literature, films, radio, dramatizations, etc.

    3. Adequately using study classes, topics, discussion groups, debates, radio, and other methods of spreading the truth about alcohol.

    4. Providing for effective poster displays which visualize the nature and effects of alcohol and the baneful results of the re-legalization of the traffic.

    5. Supporting statutes and public officials committed to the making and enforcement of laws regulating or prohibiting the use and sale of beverage alcohol.

    6. Preparing and circulating "white lists" of hotels and other public eating places in the community where alcoholic beverages are not served.

    7. Co-operating with other agencies promoting education regarding alcohol, particularly those working in the field of youth.

    8. Activity in public efforts to help to meet the menace of the rising tide of traffic accidents.

    9. Active education on the harmful effects of other narcotics (besides alcohol), especially the cigarette, with particular reference to the effects wrought among adolescent boys and among girls and women.

    10. Participation in campaigns against harmful advertising, especially for liquor and cigarettes, in magazines, billboards, newspapers, moving pictures, and on the radio.

The situation is reviewed and many suggestions are made in Dr. Poling's address. (See Chapter VI.)

Drinking Among Youth

Of course it is true that numerous young people drink. An exceptionally complete survey undertaken in a single State and involving 11,000 young people showed 54 per cent of those replying admitted some use of alcoholic beverages. A large number of those who said they do not drink admitted having no objection to drinking by others.

Except in rare cases, young people do not drink for the physical effects of alcohol. They seldom seek escape from the world in which they live—the "drowning my sorrows" motive. Youthful drinking seems to be due mostly to social pressure. Someone else does it. The crowd seems to take it for granted. Someone will "kid" you if you don't drink. Someone will leave you out of the guest list, if you won't take enough to be sociable. You can't get dates!

I suggest to Christian youth: If you don't drink and clearly state you don't, you lessen the social pressure that the drinkers put upon other young people, in any group of which you are a part or in which your customary associates participate. By providing alcohol-free recreation and social events in the community, by promoting clean athletics Christian young people quite likely do more to down the alcohol menace than by any amount of campaigning. For one of the clearest rules of substituting the "best" for the merely "good" or the downright "evil" is providing an attractive alternative.

The Allied Youth movement, a national federation of local Posts, is engaged in meeting these needs. In a youth-led, youth-officered localized program, a Post provides practical ways to get at the facts about alcohol, particularly in their immediate, nearby settings, as well as offering many opportunities for recreation, group activities, and good comradeship in a non-partisan, non-sectarian, alcohol-free program.   --W. Roy Breg

Helpful Books

"Alcohol: Its Effects on Man," Emerson.

"What's the Difference?" (Panel discussion guide), Dickerson.

"Youth Faces the Liquor Problem" (Six-chapter discussion guide, with questions, data, etc.), Davis.

Also *The Allied Youth*, alcohol education magazine for youth, published monthly.

Inquiries may be addressed to the International Society of Christian Endeavor or to Allied Youth, Inc., National Education Association Building, Washington, D. C.

Has the Church a Part?

There are two extremes accepted by some members of the church, which impede the progress of a Christian nation. The first is the attitude that the church has little to do with social problems. This idea is contradicted by "Ye are the salt of the earth." Our influence is supposed to run throughout all life, individual, family, and national. The second is that the Christian faith should fit into a system. But we are not of the world! We cannot merge Christian faith and social system *until* the system is Christianized, and we must help in the process of Christianizing.

Christian Endeavor, by no means uniform, has uniform purposes. Already Christian Endeavor has taken an active part in States as far apart geographically as Georgia and Iowa in constructive work on the liquor question.

                                        --Betty Cooper

See Chapter IV, for a complete statement on race prejudice, by Mrs. Balm.

D. Promotion of the principles of Christian patriotism.

    1. Study classes and discussion courses to discover the basic elements of a Christian's patriotism.

Helps for Study and Discussion

"Citizenship Ideals for Christian Youth," Davis. International Society of Christian Endeavor. A revised edition is contemplated for 1938.

"Living Religion," Hornell Hart (Abingdon Press).

"National Defense: Institutions, Concepts, Policies," Brunauer (The Woman's Press).

"Production for Use," Loeb (Basic Books).

"Christianity and Our World," Bennett (Association Press).

"Youth Action in Christian Patriotism." (International Council of Religious Education).

Section IV

Christic for Every International Crisis

*(The Christian Gospel applied to problems in international
peace and goodwill)*

A. Active support of Christian missions at home and abroad.

1. The society recognizing that inherent in Christian Endeavor is a sense of its world mission; that it cannot properly be confined by local conditions or within national or denominational limits, but reaches to all mankind in all the world.

2. Encouragement of missionary reading, through distribution of reading lists, circulation of missionary books, subscriptions for missionary magazines, and similar methods.

3. Adequate preparation for missionary meetings, with the use of dramatizations, films, stories, and missionary speakers.

4. Definite financial contributions to denominational and interdenominational missionary activities. (The sum of $25 contributed by any individual, society, or union will support for one day the entire foreign work of Christian Endeavor, as carried on by the World's Christian Endeavor Union, 41 Mount Vernon Street, Boston, Massachusetts.)

Jesus Meeting All Needs

Jesus in His ministry met all human needs—food, clothing, the healing of body and mind, religious instruction, guidance of man toward peace with his fellows. He was concerned foremost with the welfare of God's children, not regarding who they were or what they were or who their parents were. We must love God before we can love our fellow men or minister effectively to them.

—Myron T. Hopper

Improving Missionary Meetings

Avoid sleeping potions—paint pictures always, word pictures. God sent a picture; they saw Him in Jesus Christ.

Use catchy titles for the meetings, titles that do not tell everything. We mount to heaven on wings of surprise, so use them. For example:

"They Starve That We May Eat" (Migrant work). "Ruth Gleaned Where the Reapers Had Been." "You Are God's Farm" (Rural Missions). "Kicking over the Traces" (Changing chemistry of America's farms). "Old Lamps for New" (Missions in Turkey).

Make use of poems and songs. Know Carl Sandburg's "Songs."

Don't be boring—so use the dictionary freely, and find new words for some of the old ones you have been using in missionary education.

Missions should be generously in the society's budget. Promote missions giving by plays, such as "The Years Ahead."

Biographies are helpful. We should know the people who made missions and how they have struggled to represent *us* in carrying out Christ's great commission to preach the Gospel.

Norma Dunning

Helpful Books

"What is This Moslem World?" Watson.
"World Peace and Christian Missions." Fey.
"The Young Moslem Looks at Life." Titus.
"Highland Heritage." White.
"Out of Africa." Ross.
"Rebuilding Rural America." Dawber.
"The Story of the American Negro." Brown.
"Consider Africa." Mathews.

How Societies Help

A particularly interesting missionary meeting may be reproduced on occasion for adult groups in the church.

The Christian Endeavor societies of a church may make themselves responsible for the hospitality and entertainment of a visiting missionary.

One society having the use of a portable motion picture projector aided its denomination throughout a wide area by supplying the machine, an operator, a musician, and a lecturer-announcer to present missionary films at churches and church schools.

The missionary emphasis may be frequently applied to other topics than those deliberately labeled "missionary" by an alert committee in the society and in the union. The close connection between missionary work and world peace is obvious. The latter should not be discussed seriously by Christian groups without adequate consideration of the former. Missionary activities are so closely connected also with world health, economic justice, the democratic spirit, education, and training in Christian living that there are instances to be found in the mission fields relating to almost every topic the society considers in its year's work.

B. Promotion of the unique World Peace Fellowship of Christian Endeavor—an enrollment of Endeavorers and all friends of peace, for study and concerted action on current strategic points in the cause of peace.

For information and enrollment blanks write to the International Society of Christian Endeavor, 41 Mount Vernon Street, Boston, Massachusetts.

C. Promotion of the spirit of brotherhood and friendliness, overcoming selfish nationalism.

1. The society making studies in appreciation of the contributions of other nations to the culture, art, science, religion, invention, and music of the world.

2. Circulating the best and most recent books and other literature concerning peace and the ways to attain it.

3. Encouraging friendship projects as aids to peace: e.g., goodwill tours, holiday or visitation homes or hostels, international correspondence.

4. Participating in international travel and international gatherings by means of which are shared ideals in education, health, recreation, morals, and religion.

5. Co-operating with other agencies that promote justice among the nations; that oppose war as a means of settling disputes; that foster the words and spirit of Jesus Christ as supreme in matters of international understanding.

6. Promoting and observing annually the World Day of Prayer as a means of co-operation in brotherhood and goodwill.

The War Situation

War is taking shape along three lines: between major conflicting nations, between political and economic orders, and between philosophies.

National strife is likely to be turned into civil strife in "the next World War." The European situation as between Communism and Fascism, with Democracy practically crowded out of the conflict, is indicative.

What shall Christians do?

They may practice Christ's principles between individuals and in family life. They will seek to know other peoples better, throwing their influence toward understanding the other country, for hate is born of ignorance and misrepresentation. We should raise the level and aid the growth of the foreign-born people in our midst. Books, visitors, letters, from the other nationals should be welcomed.

Christian Endeavorers meet the war situation head on, when they talk against war in the Christian Endeavor society Sunday evening and are asked to shoulder a gun and drill with the students' training-corps on Monday.

If we are Christians, that means we must be different. We can't compromise on these matters.

—Ivan M. Gould

A Series of Meetings

Dr. Raymond M. Veh suggests a six-part discussion unit on war and peace, along the following lines:

First: Cost of war. Second: Causes of war. Third: War debts and disarmament. Fourth: Growth of the dream of World Peace. Fifth: Issues and danger spots in the world, and their relation to competitive armaments. Sixth: Christ and war.

Dramas and pageants available include: "Peace I Give to You," Wilson; "The Lord's Prayer," Coppe; "The Terrible Meek," Kennedy.

These are forms of peace demonstrations: Students' peace strikes; parades; peace mass meetings; protests to congressmen, the movie industry, newspapers; Dr. Albert W. Palmer's suggestion for a pledge at the altar of the church to refrain from bearing arms.

"Our missionary program will be useless in the next generation unless we can abolish war."

How Unions Help

Be in touch with the Emergency Peace Campaign, the National Peace Conference, and the various organizations sponsoring peace education and peace action that are included in these programs. Membership in the World Peace Fellowship of Christian Endeavor—a truly international enrollment—will give access to many such materials.

The pamphlets published by the National Peace Conference, Foreign Policy Association, National Council for the Prevention of War, and Federal Council of Churches (Department of International Justice and Good Will) are of particular value for a central reading-room or library collection on peace issues. The Committee on Militarism in Education keeps closely in touch with a situation directly affecting thousands of young people. Additional help may be secured from the International Society of Christian Endeavor and from the pages of *The Christian Endeavor World*.

The union's promotional and publicity facilities should be at the disposal of peace education forces in the community. Christian Endeavor unions are frequently represented in committees formed to carry on a united form of peace education in city or county.

* * * *

In Chapter II will be found the complete text of the peace address of Admiral Byrd.

UNITED CHRISTIAN YOUTH MOVEMENT

"Christian Youth Building a New World"

The following materials are now available for young people and their leaders:

Forward Together, a leaflet for general circulation to create interest in the movement. 1 cent each. 75 cents a hundred.

Group Action in Building a New World, a guide for local groups. 15 cents.

General Guide to Youth Action, 25 cents.

Youth Action in Personal Religious Living, 15 cents.

Youth Action in Building a Warless World, 15 cents.

Youth Action on the Liquor Problem, 15 cents.

Youth Action on the Economic Problem, 15 cents.

Youth Action in the Use of Leisure Time, 15 cents.

Youth Action in Breaking Down Barriers, 15 cents.

Youth Action in Preparing for Marriage and Home Life, 15 cents.

Youth Action in Christian Patriotism, 15 cents.

Christian Youth in Missionary Action, 15 cents.

* * *

The Christian Endeavor World, monthly journal of the International Society, is the indispensable aid for society and union workers. Its columns of news, methods, organization helps, monthly program emphases and materials for the society devotional meetings are without parallel. It contains complete treatment of the topics for Young People's, Intermediate, and Junior societies. The price is only $1.00 a year ($1.50 in Canada, $2.00 in foreign countries).

Any of these may be obtained at the prices quoted from The International Society of Christian Endeavor, 41 Mount Vernon St., Boston, Massachusetts.

www.ingramcontent.com/pod-product-compliance
Lightning Source LLC
Chambersburg PA
CBHW020949030426
42339CB00004B/17